Making Work Pay

Making Work Pay

■

America After Welfare

A READER FROM *THE AMERICAN PROSPECT*

Edited by
Robert Kuttner

THE NEW PRESS   NEW YORK

All articles originally appeared in *The American Prospect* Vol. 11 No. 15,
June 19–July 3, 2000, except Nancy Folbre, "Leave No Child Behind?,"
Janet C. Gornick and Marcia K. Meyers, "Support for Working Families,"
and Jared Bernstein and Mark Greenberg, "Reforming Welfare Reform,"
which appeared in *The American Prospect* Vol. 12 No. 1, January 1–15, 2001.

Published in the United States by The New Press, New York, 2002
Distributed by W. W. Norton & Company, Inc., New York

ISBN 1-56584-695-8 (pbk.)
CIP data available

The New Press was established in 1990 as a not-for-profit alternative to the large,
commercial publishing houses currently dominating the book publishing industry.
The New Press operates in the public interest rather than for private gain, and is
committed to publishing, in innovative ways, works of educational, cultural,
and community value that are often deemed insufficiently profitable.

The New Press, 450 West 41st Street, 6th floor, New York, NY 10036
www.thenewpress.com

Printed in Canada

2   4   6   8   10   9   7   5   3   1

Contents

Introduction: Working Principles

From Ending Welfare to Rewarding Work

ROBERT B. REICH

The cabinet met with President Bill Clinton in the Roosevelt Room of the White House on a sultry day in the summer of 1996. Many of us recommended that he not sign the welfare bill that the Republican Congress had sent him (the third one it had sent, only slightly less punitive than the first two, which he had vetoed). But an election was on the horizon, and the president's political advisers urged him to sign, lest Robert Dole use the president's timidity as a battering ram.

In the end, he did sign, of course, and since then he and many Democrats have celebrated the decline in America's welfare rolls without acknowledging that millions of people who are now at work but had been on welfare are not earning enough to support their families, that they are in dead-end jobs without a future, and that the greater harm will come when the economy slows and they will no longer be able to find work.

This book is about "making work pay," which was to have been one of the prerequisites for genuine welfare reform. The phrase originated with my friend and former colleague David Ellwood, a professor at Harvard's Kennedy School of Government, and was popularized by Bill Clinton in his 1992 presidential campaign, when he called for an end to "welfare as we know it."

It resonated with Bill Clinton's own campaign pledge from 1992 that if you worked full time, you wouldn't be poor. But like other ideas that have had the misfortune of becoming political slogans, "making work pay" went from obscurity to meaninglessness without any intervening period of coherence. The following essays seek not only to restore coherence to the original notion but also to update it for the new century.

First, some background. In America work is a citizen's most fundamental economic responsibility. It is the essence of the Protestant ethic, the criterion for being considered a "deserving" member of society. Once this responsibility is fulfilled, the burden shifts back to society.

Three Moral Commitments

To the extent that there's a moral core to American capitalism, it consists of three promises based on an individual's willingness to work. You won't find them written anywhere, but they're bedrock American values: First, any adult needing to work full time deserves a full-time job. Second, that job should pay enough to lift that person and his or her family out of poverty. Third, people should have the opportunity to move beyond this bare minimum by making full use of their talents and abilities.

On these three promises rests almost every aspect of the modern social contract that still survives. Even the moral basis for welfare reform was based on them. Any possibility for strengthening the social contract and widening the circle of prosperity depends on further redeeming them.

Consider the first: Any adult able and willing to work full time deserves a full-time job. A high rate of unemployment is bad not only because it means the nation is wasting a lot of its human resources, but also because it signals a failure on the part of society. American society does not fault someone who is actively looking for a job if none is available. The fault lies with the economy. To the extent that public policies affect the economy, society is letting these people down.

This widely accepted principle should frame future public debate about macroeconomic policy. Now that federal spending no longer has any practical consequence for stimulating the economy—both parties are committed to balancing the federal budget—the decision about how much joblessness to tolerate, and at what price, lies solely with the Federal Reserve Board's Open Market Committee. Even accepting the proposition that inflation is bad for everyone in the long term, Fed policy makers still have a great deal of discretion. They can decide whether to move aggressively to "preempt" inflation by raising short-term interest rates, thus pushing many people out of jobs, or to err on the side of allowing the economy to grow buoyantly, creating more jobs and lower unemployment, even at the risk of some inflation.

The public must understand that the Fed's decisions about when and how hard to fight inflation are profoundly distributive. The people who are most likely to be drafted into the inflation fight are at the end of most job queues. They tend to be relatively uneducated and unskilled, only marginally connected to the labor market, and poor. By the same token, these are the people most likely to move from joblessness to a job when the economy grows quickly and the labor market tightens.

Public debate should also focus on the inconsistency between a welfare system that now strictly limits individuals to five years of lifetime eligibility and a macroeconomic policy in the hands of a Federal Reserve Board bent on fighting inflation. "New economy" gurus to the contrary notwithstanding, the business cycle hasn't been repealed. Many poor people will endure several business cycles during their lifetimes featuring periods of relatively high unemployment, yet the new welfare system makes no allowance for this. America hasn't succumbed to a recession since the new welfare law was put into effect, but undoubtedly the Fed eventually will raise interest rates until the economy slows. The landing may be hard or soft, but it will be a landing in any event, and unemployment will rise.

Unemployment insurance is not nearly up to the task. States have tightened eligibility for unemployment insurance to the point where only one in three people who are temporarily unemployed qualifies. If we continue with the new welfare system and don't do anything to expand unemployment insurance, and if most Americans would be troubled to find large numbers of poor families on the streets, the nation will have no choice but to provide a significant number of public-service jobs. Public-service employment raises a number of hard questions, of course. How diligently must people search for full-time jobs without success in order to be eligible for such jobs? What sort of public-service job qualifies as real work as opposed to morally questionable "make work"? What should these jobs pay, and should workers within them be allowed to unionize? Yet the moral imperative that anyone able and willing to work deserves a full-time job logically requires the creation of such jobs or else abandonment of the strict time limits contained within the new welfare law.

A Living Wage

Consider the second promise: A job should pay enough to bring a worker and his or her family out of poverty. The one clearly positive consequence of welfare reform has been to move several million people from being considered "undeserving poor" because they don't work to being viewed as "deserving" poor because they do. Most former welfare recipients are as poor as they were before, but the fact that they now work for their meager living has altered the politics surrounding the question of what to do about their poverty, because it has sharply raised the second moral tenet of capitalism.

Thus has the minimum wage become more salient. When I came to Washington at the start of 1993, Democrats didn't want to talk about raising the minimum wage (and Bill Clinton didn't want to get near the issue) because it was seen as something that "old" Democrats worried about. Its real monetary value had eroded for years, and the poor workers who directly benefited from it were politically inactive. Yet as welfare reform came closer to becoming a political certainty, the moral argument for a higher minimum wage gained credence. How could America in good conscience expect millions of welfare recipients to work for a living if they couldn't earn enough to live on? By the time the Republican-controlled Congress tried to block passage of a minimum-wage increase in 1996, public-opinion polls showed that 80 to 85 percent of Americans were in favor of raising it, even though the vast majority of people who were polled would be unaffected. With a presidential election looming, the Republicans had no choice but to get out of the way. As the 2000 election loomed, Republicans successfully warded off an election-year push by the Democrats to seek another increase in the minimum wage. Two bills currently wait in Congress that propose to raise the wage by $1.00 over three years.

A sensible approach would be to raise the minimum wage to its historic level—roughly half the median wage (which would put it at about $7 an hour)—and thereafter index it to the median wage. When combined with the Earned Income Tax Credit (EITC)—now the biggest antipoverty program in the federal government—and with food stamps, this higher minimum wage would lift a family of two children and one full-time adult worker out of poverty. Of course, the official poverty line drastically understates the true needs of a typical family; it was calculated in the mid-1960s, when a family could survive on a budget totaling about three times the cost of feeding itself adequately. Since then, housing and health care costs have soared. If a family is unable to secure housing assistance or Medicaid, it can be technically above the poverty line yet still be deeply impoverished.

How else to ensure that a full-time worker earns enough? The other options pose tricky problems. Making the minimum wage a "living" wage—at $10 or more an hour—could deter employers from hiring many low-skilled workers; the employers would sooner substitute automated machinery or not have the work done at all. Alternatively, expanding the EITC to cover the gap might deter employers from paying their workers adequately, knowing that taxpayers would make up the difference. We don't know exactly how high the minimum wage could be raised or how far the EITC could be expanded without causing these undesirable results, so there's room to experiment. And experiment we should.

Unionization fills in another piece of the puzzle. Although it's difficult to unionize low-wage workers—they tend to work in small establishments and are easily intimidated by employers who don't want unions—the fact that most low-wage workers are in the local service economy means their jobs won't drift abroad if employers have to pay more for them. And recent successes in unionizing health-care workers in California and in conducting a national campaign to lift the wages of janitors suggest larger possibilities ahead. But here, too, we eventually run into the same economic wall. As with the minimum wage, there's a limit to how high unionized wages can go before employers find it cheaper to automate the jobs, cut back on staffing, or not offer the services to begin with.

The key to making work pay is encouraging employers to pay higher wages to people at the bottom. This would happen if the Fed allowed the economy to grow so fast that demand for low-wage workers exceeded the supply, with the result that their wages were bid upward. This strategy would take us only so far; as noted, at some point it would ignite inflation. The nation might also try to limit the influx of low-wage immigrants, whose ready availability in certain large urban areas has depressed the wages of low-income workers already there. Finally, we could ensure that everyone had an education sufficient to raise their productivity and thereby warrant higher pay. This is a good and noble goal, worth pursuing. The problem is, there's no magic formula for accomplishing it. And even if we succeed, the beneficial results are years away.

Separately, none of these measures will suffice. Together—a somewhat higher minimum wage, a somewhat expanded EITC, more unionization of low-wage workers, lower short-term interest rates, faster growth, some limits on low-skilled immigration, and better education—they probably could lift full-time working families out of poverty, with few or no negative effects. We don't know the ideal combination of these measures, but the nation is surely rich enough and clever enough to try until we get it right.

Talent, Education, and Making It in America

Finally, the third promise: All workers should be allowed to get ahead by making full use of their talents and abilities. Here again, there is broad consensus, and it has existed for a long time. This was the basic argument underlying the free school movement of the nineteenth century, the high school movement of the early twentieth, and the vast expansion of public universities after World War II. It should now be the basic argument for ensuring that a good system of education and job training be available to all Americans, not just those who are better off. And it should be the grounds for arguing against state welfare schemes now requiring that former recipients go to work immediately—that they "work first" rather than gain additional skills enabling them to secure better jobs.

The original welfare bill that quietly emerged from the innards of Bill Clinton's own administration called not only for a higher minimum wage and expanded EITC to make work pay, but also for a system of supports to give people the capacity to stay employed and build their futures. Job training was included. In addition, there was provision for health care: If moving from welfare to work meant a loss of Medicaid benefits, the journey would be perilous. Transportation assistance (or a good infrastructure of public transit) was also assumed to be necessary, because poverty is becoming more concentrated geographically in areas where there are few if any jobs, while most of the job growth is occurring in suburban rings. The cost and time entailed in getting from home to work and back again puts an especially onerous burden on the poor. An allowance for child care was in the original bill as well, in recognition of the fact that poor mothers could not otherwise afford decent care for their young children.

Needless to say, none of these supports made it to the bill that the president eventually signed. Together with an expanded EITC, they would have cost several billion dollars more than the total cost of welfare at the time, which was assumed by the White House to be a political nonstarter. And yet, 70 percent of welfare recipients were even then managing to get off welfare and into a job. Their problem was remaining in the job. Without such supports, most of them fell back into welfare. We do not know exactly how many of the people who are no longer collecting welfare are still working productively, but it seems a safe bet to say that without these supports and without adequate training and education, they will not remain at work for very long. At best, they're in jobs with no real possibility for promotion.

Almost all states now have sizable surpluses in the funding they receive from the federal government to cover welfare "reform." They should be using these surpluses for child care and other work supports. Instead, they're using the surpluses for tax cuts and highways.

Welfare had become deeply unpopular in America partly because of race. Even though more recipients were white than black, it was viewed by most Americans as a program for "them." But welfare had also lost legitimacy among America's blue- and pink-collar workers, because they did not see why they should suffer economic hardship while people poorer than they were appeared to get a free ride. Starting in the 1970s, the loss of manufacturing jobs required many women to work in order to maintain family incomes that previously had been sustained by one male worker; many of these women were mothers of young children. These families saw no reason that women who were only slightly poorer than themselves should be able to stay home with their children and receive welfare benefits.

But now that all struggling Americans are more or less in the same sinking boat, there's less reason for working-class families to resent the poor. It is now possible to argue that all people on the bottom half of the income ladder should have access to better education and training, health care, transportation, and child care if they're going to be able to get ahead.

In fact, it is possible to redeem all three of the promises implicit within the American social compact. There are now only "deserving" working people, many of them very poor, along with the disabled who cannot work. There is thus an opportunity to build a new structure of social responsibility upon the foundation stones of our common morality. Regardless of who you are, if you need a job, you should have one; your work should pay you enough to lift you and your family out of poverty; and you should have an opportunity to make the most of your talents and abilities. That there is widespread agreement on these basics brings us more than halfway home. To get the rest of the way, we will need a politics that puts these principles to work.

What does it take to make work pay? This collection suggests that it takes many things: welfare policy designed not just to cut the rolls but to reward work; stronger unions; a better-designed EITC; and more effec-

tive wage regulation. It takes high-quality child care and smarter training programs. Reading these essays, one appreciates that the elements of
such a national policy are already in place, though piecemeal, and that
the country could easily afford a national commitment to make work
pay. What's lacking is the political will.

Making Work Pay

A Clean Sweep

The SEIU's Organizing Drive for Janitors
Shows How Unionization Can Raise Wages

HAROLD MEYERSON

On Friday, April 7, 2000, I came upon one method of increasing the income of the working poor that, I confess, had never even occurred to me. The janitors of Service Employees International Union (SEIU) Local 1877, embroiled in a countywide strike, were marching down Wilshire Boulevard from downtown Los Angeles to tony Century City, roughly an eight-mile walk. Ten years earlier, another such march had culminated in one of the LAPD's periodic riots, when police set upon the marchers in Century City, beating and injuring scores. This time, L.A.'s city attorney was in the parade's front row, flanked by a dozen other elected officials, Jesse Jackson, and a host of ministers, priests, and rabbis. But that wasn't all that was different about this march.

As the janitors left downtown, the people on the sidewalks—few of whom had known in advance about the march—started giving them a thumbs-up sign. After a couple of miles, the sidewalk passersby weren't just signaling their support; they were cheering. Then, as the march reached Beverly Hills, the people on the sidewalks—first one, then a couple, then a bunch—did something I'd never seen. They darted into the street and handed the janitors cash. Spontaneous redistribution—something never before noted in any recorded history of Los Angeles.

Seventeen days later, L.A.'s janitors won themselves a considerable nonspontaneous redistribution: a wage increase of about 26 percent, spread over the next three years. The janitors who work at either end of the march—downtown or in Century City, areas almost entirely unionized—will see their hourly pay rise from just under $8 to just over $10. (At that rate, it's possible that one parent in a two-working-parent family could afford to work just one job—and actually get some time with his or her kids.) Janitors in other, less unionized parts of town will see an even greater percentage increase.

The far greater miracle, of course, was this: that a union whose members are 98 percent immigrants—80 percent Central Americans, 55 percent women, and all of them poor—could wrest this kind of settlement from the nation's largest building service contractors and real estate investors. The settlement is a tribute to the spirit and tenacity of the janitors themselves, to the cohesiveness of the L.A. labor movement, and to the manifest strategic smarts of the international union to which the janitors belong, the SEIU. The settlement, so to speak, is the result of a three-level exceptionalism: the local, the central labor council, and the international are each about as good as it gets in the American labor movement today.

From which follows a depressing corollary: The vast majority of American unions, at all levels, have yet to make a dent in the growing problem of low-wage work. Unionizing the workers in sweatshops, for instance, has proven all but impossible, as contractors routinely threaten to move the work to a Third World nation (and routinely do). In industries that can't flee—service, transport, health care, and tourism—unionizing the workforce has been possible, but only by dint of extraordinary efforts.

Who Organizes?

Since 1995, when John Sweeney won the presidency of the AFL-CIO on a platform that emphasized organizing above all else, a number of major internationals have done just that—and have genuine membership growth to show for it. Unfortunately, that number is roughly ten out of the sixty-eight unions that belong to the federation.

Some among the Organizing Ten have focused their efforts on low-wage workers. The Union of Needletrades, Industrial and Textile Employees (UNITE!) has had major breakthroughs in the organizing of textile and nursing home workers; the Hotel Employees and Restaurant Employees (HERE) union has won excellent contracts for previously low-wage hotel employees; the American Federation of State, County and Municipal Employees (AFSCME) has launched a major drive to organize Head Start workers. By every measure, though, the union with the greatest success at organizing low-wage workers is the SEIU. In recent years, the Service Employees have unionized well over 100,000 home health-care workers and nursing home workers. It is currently waging campaigns to organize security screeners at airports, many of whom work at the minimum wage.

But the SEIU's signature campaign has been its Justice for Janitors effort. Initiated in 1985 during John Sweeney's tenure as SEIU president, J for J has become known throughout the country as one of the most noisy, rambunctious, disruptive—and successful—efforts both to organize and to win raises for workers at or near the bottom of the economy. Indeed, one such disruption—a rush-hour sit-down blocking one of the bridges across the Potomac River in Washington, D.C., pulled off under the very noses of the police detail assigned to guard the bridge—became a major point of contention between Sweeney and Tom Donahue, who was Sweeney's opponent during the 1995 campaign for the AFL-CIO presidency. The role of labor, Donahue insisted, was to build bridges, not block them. Sweeney countered that he'd built as many bridges as anyone in the labor movement, but there was a time to block bridges, too: when management was recalcitrant. It wasn't nice—it infuriated motorists—but, then, the janitors have never depended on the kindness of strangers. More than any other union, the SEIU—under both Sweeney and his successor, Andy Stern—has understood that the only real power of the poor is the power to disrupt. And no other union has channeled that disruption in so brilliant and productive a way.

A number of the SEIU's campaigns to organize low-income workers, of course, have yet to yield anything, and the gains the union has won at the table for many of the low-wage workers it has organized have been modest. But the union has also known some sterling successes, and the campaign that the L.A. janitors waged in the spring of 2000 stands out as one of those rare moments in contemporary unionism when virtually everything clicked. It's an object lesson in how a union can transform the living standards, and the lives, of the working poor. But it's also an illustration of just how daunting that task really is.

At first glance, the very idea that L.A.'s janitors could sustain and win a strike seemed preposterous. With an average hourly wage of

$7.20, they were in no position to have socked away a rainy-day fund. The fact that they were spread across roughly 900 different work sites meant that bonding together as an effective union was anything but easy; it also made setting up effective picket lines very difficult. (The local has 8,500 members.) The fragmented and byzantine structure of the industry also complicated matters greatly, compelling the union to negotiate up front with eighteen different building service contractors while conducting back-channel discussions with a like number of building owners. In this kind of structure, the least wealthy, or most stingy, service contractor could easily gum up a settlement.

The primary asset the janitors brought to their strike, of course, the sine qua non of their victory, was their local, which had taken them a dozen years to rebuild to a position of strength. Until 1983–84, Los Angeles, like most non-Southern U.S. cities, had a unionized janitorial workforce (which in Los Angeles was heavily black). In 1983 the local signed a contract with the service contractors providing its members with an hourly wage of $7.32.

At the same time, thousands of Central Americans began moving to Los Angeles, many fleeing the U.S.-backed wars that were raging in their homelands. Building service contractors began discharging their unionized workers and hiring refugees. No other American city experienced quite so wholesale a substitution of one workforce for another. None of L.A.'s new janitors made anything like $7.32 an hour. Instead, they made the federal minimum wage—then $3.35 an hour, just 44 percent of the rate set by the union contract. "Almost immediately after the ink was dry on the contract," says Jono Shaffer, who came to L.A. to start up Justice for Janitors a few years later, "the union had to go into renegotiations, dropping wages just to keep some members in the buildings." From 5,000 members in 1978, the local shrank to 1,800 in 1985.

Throughout the mid-1980s, many of the SEIU's janitorial locals were under assault from contractors either able to exploit a changing workforce or just indulging in the rampant union-busting of the time. In 1985 the union hastily assembled its first, impromptu Justice for Janitors campaign in Pittsburgh, where management was trying to win major givebacks. In 1986 SEIU decided to shore up its position in building services by making J for J a national—and proactive rather than reactive—campaign. After an initial victory in Denver, J for J came to Los Angeles in 1988.

Reorganizing the L.A. local proved particularly arduous. "In a sense," Shaffer recalls, "the new local began on the Olympic Boulevard bus from Century City [home to many high-rises] to Pico Union [home to many janitors], the 2:30 A.M. bus. It was the janitors' private bus; there sure wasn't anyone else on it, and it was the one place where they were together and could talk freely about their work."

By the early 1990s, the janitors had unionized Century City, strengthened their position downtown, and formed a distinct, statewide janitors' local. With accomplished J for J organizer Mike Garcia as its new president, the local plunged into a series of campaigns organizing janitors in L.A.'s numerous suburbs and edge cities, and persuading the building contractors to recognize the union and agree to the terms of its L.A. master contract. Characteristically, these campaigns combined on-site strikes; pressure from local pols, clerics, and community groups; and the occasional intervention of the buildings' owners on the janitors' behalf. The pay scale for these newer recruits, however, lagged behind that in the downtown area and in Century City. This is a common pattern among janitors' locals, where suburban membership, like suburban high-rises, tends to be newer and less dense than in downtown areas.

What It Takes to Organize

Simply by setting up J for J, Sweeney was going where most of the rest of American labor feared to tread. The campaign required SEIU to make alliances with community groups and hire a slew of young organizers off campuses and from community-based organizations. This was far from common practice at the time, because most unions viewed such groups and organizers as too radical or because organizing was just not a union priority, or for both reasons.

The L.A. janitors' local got more than its share of such organizers, however. Together with members who'd been politically active in their homelands and had led the fight to create a distinct janitors' local, they set about building a union that involved the maximum number of members in its work and decision making (a practice at which HERE, the hotel and restaurant union, has also excelled). Over the past five years, as the local grew to represent 70 percent of the janitorial workforce in L.A.'s class-A office properties, members learned to represent one another in grievances and to lead meetings; they also mastered the arcane structure of their industry. In late March 2000, with their contract about to expire and talks with employers at an impasse, the union convened a meeting of its 100 or so stewards. There, says Triana Silton, the staffer in charge of J for J in Los Angeles, the union's leaders told the stewards, "If we go out, you folks will have to run the strike." Which, the stewards pledged, they would.

Still, any field commander about to go into battle has to feel a little nervous, and a week before the strike began, Silton called Shaffer, her predecessor. "She wanted reassurance that we weren't about to embark on a countywide strike [Los Angeles is by far the most populous county in the United States] with twenty-five people," says Shaffer. "I told her what she knew but wanted to hear anyway: We'd have a thousand." And so they did.

By day, as the newscast helicopters hovered overhead, the janitors (at times numbering well over 1,000) marched down L.A.'s boulevards and threw together rallies with the speed and mobility of Patton's Third Army. (On one occasion, they rustled up 500 members and half of L.A.'s city council on three hours' notice so that Ted Kennedy, passing through town, could endorse the strike.) At sunset, the real work of the strike began as members dispersed to the myriad office buildings around town. "With so many buildings out, you couldn't possibly have staff at more than a handful," Shaffer says. "At most work sites, the members ran the strike and the picket line and the scab patrols."

In the end, the union pulled roughly half its members onto the streets in its effort to shut down the cleanup of L.A.'s office buildings. The net the janitors strung had plenty of holes in it, but the nighttime cleanings in many of the city's most prominent buildings were incomplete and haphazard, when they happened at all.

Local 1877 had had plenty of practice mobilizing its members. In a city where labor has played the decisive role in election after election over the past four years, the janitors were the most politically active union in town. "In the election of November '98," says local president Garcia, "we turned out for 1,500 shifts [a shift means walking a precinct or working a phone bank]—more than any union." The local worked under the aegis of the Los Angeles County Federation of Labor, whose operation focuses on turning out both union members and new immigrant voters. "For this," says the group's executive secretary-treasurer Miguel Contreras, "the janitors are critical. Their members get home from their jobs at 4:00 A.M., and show up for a precinct walk at 7:00 A.M."

With the janitors as its shock troops, the Los Angeles County Federation of Labor has become the election-day powerhouse of L.A. politics. Since Contreras assumed its leadership in 1996, the federation has intervened in seventeen district races—all hotly contested, at all levels of government—and has prevailed in sixteen of them.

The federation brought its own distinct clout to the janitors' strike; combined with the janitors' own efforts, it's no mystery why Local 1877 went into the strike with a statement of support from forty-eight L.A.-area elected officials or, as the strike unfolded, why it won further statements of support from the county supervisors, both houses of the state legislature, a unanimous city council, and Republican mayor Richard Riordan. Not since the 1994 earthquake had so many L.A. elected officials come together for the same cause.

The intervention that many of these officials made on the janitors' behalf was anything but casual: Council members were arrested for civil disobedience; assembly members sat on the janitors' side of the table during bargaining sessions; congressmen addressed rallies; Ted Kennedy, Dianne Feinstein, and Al Gore came to town and spoke for their cause. Assembly speaker Antonio Villaraigosa, county supervisor Zev Yaroslavsky, and the mayor publicly and privately pressured their building-owner buddies to settle.

One factor in generating such singular solidarity among the elected officials was apparent on the day of the janitors' march, at the post-primary breakfast that the Los Angeles County Federation of Labor hosted for pols it had helped in the previous month's primary. The breakfast was held in a hotel along the janitors' parade route, so the assembled pols could come outside and bless the janitors as they passed. However, the absence of one pol—nine-term congressman Marty Martinez—was felt more than the presence of all the others. In the March primary, the federation had broken with all precedent to oppose Martinez's reelection. Martinez had a career 90 percent AFL-CIO voting record, but he was the most lackadaisical of members. Even worse, he had given his vote to the administration during the 1997 fight over Fast Track (which would have restored the president's authority to submit international trade deals to Congress for an all-or-nothing vote rather than possible amendment) in return for White House support for a freeway extension, without so much as notifying the unions that he was going to switch sides. When state senator Hilda Solis, a stellar pro-labor legislator with wide support, challenged Martinez, the federation endorsed her and poured in an army of volunteers, the greatest number of whom came from the janitors. Solis clobbered Martinez 69 to 31 percent—and the ghost of poor Marty hung over the breakfast as a grim reminder to all the electeds of the fate that might await them if they spurned the unions' cause.

Adding oomph to the janitors' clout was just one of the federation's endeavors on the janitor's behalf. In 2000, contracts expired for 300,000 of the 800,000 union members whose locals are federation affiliates, and the federation has turned the local labor movement into a kind of mutual-aid society. Even before the janitors' strike began, it convened a rally of 10,000 members from all the different unions whose contracts were up, and almost all these unions were to provide the janitors with money, food, and bodies in the weeks ahead. Locals that had long been indifferent to such struggles honored the janitors' picket lines this time around. The operating engineers—who maintain elevators, air-conditioning systems, and such in office buildings all across town—

offered full pay from their own strike fund to any members who didn't cross the janitors' lines. Before the strike, the operating engineers had never given any indication that they cared whether the janitors lived or died.

Solidarity on a Bigger Stage

The janitors' strike was not simply a local strike. The chief building-maintenance contractors they were fighting were national, even global, corporations. The companies, Real Estate Investment Trusts (REITs), and pension funds that owned L.A.'s high-rises owned high-rises all across the nation. And, accordingly, the janitors' international union had decided to turn their strike into a national one.

What the SEIU had done was line up the expiration dates of its janitorial contracts in most major cities so that, as nearly as possible, they would coincide or at least follow one another in close succession. The L.A. janitors walked first, but within two weeks they were followed by the janitors in Chicago and San Diego, at the same time that New York's janitors settled without a strike. One week after the L.A. strike ended, janitors were slated to strike in Cleveland, and so it goes, one city after another, through October.

The union is merely following the consolidation of the industry. In the 1980s, save in those cities where the unions were exceptionally strong (New York, San Francisco, downtown Chicago), building owners created a protective shield behind which they could deny all responsibility for the union-busting of the Reagan years. They handed over the task of hiring, firing, supervising, and paying the janitors to the hitherto small-scale and local building service industry. (The amounts these contractors agreed to pay the janitors, however, still had to be cleared with the building owners.) In short order, these contractors grew mightily, and soon the industry came to be dominated by such nation-wide companies as American Building Maintenance (ABM) and One-Source (until relatively recently, a Danish-based conglomerate called ISS/DESCO Services).

Moreover, the ownership of class-A office properties has also been consolidated in recent years. In the 1980s, most of downtown L.A.'s high-rises were owned by foreign (chiefly Japanese) investors. Today, the city's choice properties are owned primarily by REITs and pension funds—the same REITs and pension funds that own choice properties throughout the nation. According to an April 2000 survey in the *Los Angeles Business Journal*, 51 percent of the class-A properties on L.A.'s west side—that is, the highest-rent buildings in all of Los Angeles—were owned by pension funds and another 21 percent by REITs. Moreover, according to figures compiled by the SEIU, the largest class-A property owner in southern California is also the largest in the United States—Chicago-based Equity Investments, which owns 77 million square feet across the country. Another major L.A. real estate owner, Warren "Ned" Spiecker, has 41 million square feet of office property on the West Coast.

When L.A.'s janitors struck, then, SEIU leaders were already talking with these owners and contractors on a national level. "We met with ABM, OneSource, Equity, the major owners in New York and L.A. prior to the contract expirations," says SEIU president Andy Stern. "We made clear that these were integrated, though not common, negotiations. When we sat down with owners and contractors in Chicago or L.A.," Stern continues, "they understood that this wasn't simply a discussion about Chicago or L.A."

So did SEIU's janitors all across the nation. As the date for the first contract expiration neared, the international set up a series of teleconferences among members in different cities, members of one local flew across the country to sit in at the bargaining sessions of another local, and a nationwide solidarity developed among the janitors. (Solidarity is the concept that unions most frequently invoke and most seldom cultivate.) It was this cross-city bond that underlay the threat that the international's leaders conveyed to the owners and contractors: If the local on strike in L.A. against ABM, say, sent one picket to a building cleaned by ABM in New York, the New York janitors wouldn't clean the building. By the final week of the L.A. strike, the SEIU put this plan into action, ratcheting up the pressure. "Members from 1877 [the L.A. local] flew to Seattle, Denver, San Francisco, San Jose, and their pickets were honored," says SEIU building service director Stephen Lerner. "We just did a couple of buildings in each city for one night, but we planned to escalate considerably if the strike had to go into its fourth week."

The international's threat to the nationwide owners and employers worked because, on the management side of the table, size matters. The building owners—for whom the janitors' wages are just a small part of their overall expenses—can bring pressure on the contractors, from whom janitors' wages take a bigger bite. This is why the SEIU prefers to negotiate directly with the owners, which it's able to do only in the cities where it's strongest.

In Los Angeles, Stern says, "large numbers of the owners were much more interested in settling—and settling quickly—than the contractors." Indeed, in the final negotiations, the major building owners jointly threatened the contractors by suggesting they weren't really indispensable to performance of janitorial work. On the Thursday before the strike settled, says Rob Maguire, one of L.A.'s mega-owners, "we told them that it had to be finished by Monday and that we were prepared to enter into a separate agreement with the union if they didn't get it done."

Where buildings were owned by pension funds—many of them directed by trustees selected by the public-sector unions whose funds they invest—the international's involvement was even more direct, if less conspicuous. The two largest pension funds in the United States are CalPERS and CalSTIRS, for California's public employees and its teachers. The dominant public employee union in California happens to be the SEIU. "Clearly, a lot of calls were made by CalPERS and CalSTIRS," says one source close to the negotiations.

One other service that the SEIU performed for the janitors—and here the help came more from a consortium of California locals than from the international—was to sponsor prestrike polling and focus groups to assist 1877, and other SEIU locals facing the prospect of a strike, in honing their message. Truth be told, though, the janitors didn't need much help. From the moment they took to the streets, they plainly struck a nerve.

The most astonishing sight in the janitors' strike—and I saw it repeatedly—was of motorists stuck in traffic for fifteen or twenty minutes as the janitors marched across an intersection. Time and again, drivers got out of their cars and shook their fists—not in anger, but in clamorous support.

The strike had two immediate effects on the city. First, it pushed the reality of low-wage work smack into everyone's face. (Even L.A.'s TV newscasts—the most substance-free in the land—were compelled to cover the janitors' daily marches and mention the wage rates at which they worked.) Second, the janitors provided the city with its first plausible and visible solution for poverty-wage work: unionization. In middle-class L.A., let alone in upwards-of-middle-class L.A.,

I've not detected any overwhelming public sentiment to unionize low-wage workers. But the janitors forced Los Angeles to confront its transformation into the national capital of low-wage work on a less theoretical level. Behind the spontaneous cash donations in the streets of Beverly Hills was not only guilt about such manifest poverty in the midst of such manifest plenty, but also a kind of civic relief: At last, somebody was doing something about what Los Angeles had become—a city with a vanishing middle class and an explosion in the number of Angelenos at work for poverty-level wages.

For affluent Los Angeles, then, the strike produced an altogether unanticipated wave of civic improvement, as Charles Dickens would define civic improvement. The cardinal, whose record of support for working-class struggle has been mixed, but who performed a special Mass for the janitors and called his building-owner parishioners on their behalf, was never truer to the spirit of the Sermon on the Mount. The mayor, whose record of support for working-class struggle has been way more mixed than the cardinal's, was never more attentive to his city's deepest dilemma. The inhabitants of this First World metropolis, whose normal level of economic and political consciousness ranges from "false" to "un," were never more sensitive to, and willing to remedy, the plight of those who live there at near–Third World wages.

But what has the strike meant to the other Los Angeles, the one from which the janitors come? How, if at all, has it altered the prospects for organizing?

Los Angeles may be one of the nation's most diverse metropolises, but what happened to the demographics of building maintenance in the 1980s happened to virtually all of blue-collar Los Angeles. At the dawn of this new century, the Los Angeles working class is almost entirely Latino. And of Latinos' affinity for unions, there can be no doubt (most particularly in Los Angeles, where labor is Latino-led and the most visible locals are Latino-dominated). Proposition 226, the 1998 initiative that would have greatly curtailed union's political activity, was rejected by state Latino voters by a 75 to 25 percent margin. Black voters didn't reject it that decisively, nor did union members.

But if pro-union sentiment were sufficient to create a unionized workplace, the rate of unionization in the United States would be closer to one-third than its current 14 percent. To the nonunion sector of the L.A. working class (that is, virtually all of it), the janitors' strike can be viewed in two ways. "This strike can both scare immigrants and inspire them," says Maria Elena Durazo, leader of the only local union in town (HERE Local 11) with a record of immigrant organizing, collective bargaining, and political participation comparable to that of the janitors. "It can be daunting. It all depends on what the respective unions do in their industries. Do we do the day-to-day work of challenging and developing immigrant workers [to become activists and leaders] in their workplaces? If we don't, the strike on its own won't inspire a whole spontaneous movement. It takes a particular kind of union, with tough organizers and a tough organizing program."

The SEIU's commitment to such "tough" organizing is unrivaled in the labor movement. When Sweeney was president, the union was spending nearly a third of its budget on organizing, at a time when the average for almost every other union was about 2 percent. Under Stern, the cut for organizing has risen to 47 percent, requiring the international to reduce, and in a few cases eliminate, some of its departments. Even among the Organizing Ten, it's only in the SEIU that the organizers clearly outnumber everyone else on staff. The international has also set targets for its locals: In the first year of the program, it encouraged them to spend 10 percent of their resources on organizing; in the second year, 15 percent; in the third year, 20 percent. It also provided locals with the assistance to make that transition.

The service employees' leaders are still raising the ante. At its 2000 convention, the SEIU voted for a dues increase to establish new nationwide funds for organizing and bargaining in specific sectors. "The next time the building service contracts come up, in 2003, imagine what we could do if we had $10 million to supplement what the locals have set aside," says Stern. "Imagine what it could mean for organizing, too. This nationwide approach has long been common for industrial unions, but the strategy can also be applied to Hilton and Starwood [hotels], to hospital chains and nursing home chains, and to building services."

This is exactly the kind of proposal that most unions have tended to avoid, at least since Walter Reuther's day. It asks the members to pay more today, or give up a level of servicing to which they're accustomed, for a program that may produce more organizing—and, thus, greater union density in their sector or locale and, thus, maybe, better wage settlements—in the future. John Wilhelm won wide acceptance for this kind of trade-off when he ran the HERE local in Las Vegas, as it grew from 15,000 members to nearly 60,000. But it's relatively easy to understand concepts like union density and its relation to wage scales in a one-industry town surrounded by 300 miles of desert. The SEIU's members are being asked to make such a trade-off when things like union density and its relation to wages are harder to see. The union leaders figure that the success of the newly coordinated janitor strikes will help them make their point.

Outside the SEIU, HERE, UNITE!, and a handful of other unions, however, this level of commitment to and strategic thinking about organizing is not yet evident. Over the past half-decade in Los Angeles, organizing drives have fizzled for lack of the kind of corporate strategy that the SEIU brought to its building service division, or for failure of long-established locals to activate their members in organizing new ones.

Organizing the New Labor Force

Meanwhile, the janitor and hotel worker unions are beginning to assume within L.A.'s immigrant community the kind of full-service tribune role that the garment unions played in the immigrant communities of New York in the early twentieth century. Indeed, merely to meet their members' needs, these unions cannot bargain simply for wages and benefits. HERE Local 11 won a groundbreaking provision in its last contract that gives hotel workers a full year to return to their jobs with their seniority intact in the event that the Immigration and Naturalization Service (INS) deports them, and that requires the hotel to reemploy them if they can come back within a two-year period. The janitors won a similar, though considerably more modest, provision in their new contract.

In 2000, both the SEIU and HERE took the lead in persuading the national AFL-CIO to rescind its long-standing support for sanctions against businesses that employ illegal immigrants. That February, the labor federation's executive council unanimously adopted the call for a broad new amnesty for millions of undocumented workers, and for the repeal of the so-called employer sanctions law of 1986.

Both the SEIU and HERE took the lead in persuading the national AFL-CIO to rescind its long-standing support for sanctions against businesses that employ undocumented immigrants. The AFL-CIO conducted a series of hearings around the country on the question of whether there should be a new amnesty for illegals, and in February, the labor federation's executive council unanimously adopted the position. Amnesty is a very practical concern for virtually all unions that organize, since the rank-and-file leaders of their drives—not just in Los Angeles, and not only among janitors—are increasingly immigrants, whom, increasingly, the INS is deporting. But amnesty's appeal reaches far beyond the unions' ranks, and Mike Garcia took the occasion of the janitors' contract ratification vote—covered by a swarm of Spanish-language newscasts and newspapers—to announce that the union's next major battle would be for the new amnesty.

The strike has confirmed a new order in the political firmament of Latino California. The janitors, in tandem with the hotel workers, have supplanted the United Farm Workers (UFW) as the political power-house and moral beacon of local Latino politics. Twenty-five years ago, the UFW and its allies walked more precincts in Latino L.A. than anyone else, cultivated the support of governors and senators, and came to symbolize the entire Latino (in those days, it was "Chicano") cause. Today, it's the janitors who walk the most precincts, who've amassed the broadest political backing, who've caught the imagination and won the allegiance of this new, larger immigrant community—that is, of L.A.'s working class. One index of this charge: By the strike's second week, people were buying the janitors' signature red T-shirts off their backs; by the third week, knockoffs of the T-shirts began popping up in the garment district. Another index: Throughout the strike, L.A.'s more nationalistic Latino officials, whose candidates the janitors have opposed and defeated in election after election, nonetheless felt compelled to come to the janitors' rallies. To have been missing in action, or deemed insufficiently pro-janitor, would have amounted to political suicide.

Such is the decay of the laws protecting organizing, and of most unions' capacity to organize, that the janitors' stunning success is no guarantee that organizing in Los Angeles will pick up—much less that the silver bullet has been found for the travails of the city's low-wage earners. Then again, my *LA Weekly* colleague Joseph Trevino tells me he stopped by a meeting in the Latino neighborhood of Lincoln Heights about a week after the strike ended. Citizens for a Better Environment, a group that organizes in L.A.'s nonwhite working-class communities, had convened the meeting to build support for a campaign to expose the neighborhood's high rates of cancer. As the meeting went on, as the participants grew more animated, the talk was increasingly of the janitors, some of whom lived right down the block: of the dedication they'd shown, the example they'd provided, the standard they'd set for the entire community. Abruptly, the spirit of the meeting was that of the janitors' battle cry, that old UFW slogan they had made credible for a new generation: *Sí, se puede* (Yes, we can do it). Maybe they can.

Ending Poverty as We Know It

MICHAEL MASSING

In 1999, when a magazine editor asked me to write about the progress of welfare reform in America, I called around to see which state was leading the way. I ended up in Wisconsin. Under the direction of Republican governor Tommy Thompson, Wisconsin had begun cutting its rolls earlier than most other states and had pared them far more sharply. During my visit there, almost everyone I met embraced the idea of welfare reform. Even longtime advocates for the poor said they had become convinced that too many people had become too dependent on welfare and that reform had given them a needed push.

But I also heard many complaints about how welfare reform was being carried out. Thousands of people who were unable to work were being pushed off the rolls; hunger and homelessness had increased. Even those who had found jobs were having trouble retaining them, and their average wage was falling. Welfare reform was getting many people off the dole, I was told; it was not getting them out of poverty.

Increasingly, this is the national story. Since 1996, when President

Clinton signed the Personal Responsibility and Work Opportunity Reconciliation Act, the nation's welfare rolls have declined 43 percent. Most of those who left have found jobs and, in this (until recently) robust economy, most work has paid above minimum wage. But not by much. Many welfare leavers have become trapped in the Death Valley of the job market, working as janitors and clerks, child-care workers and nursing home assistants. A study issued in 1999 by the Urban Institute found that people leaving welfare were experiencing the same low wages and job insecurity as low-income mothers who had not been on welfare. This, the institute stated, "suggests that policies to encourage and support work might usefully be focused more generally on low-income families with children rather than directing services specifically to former welfare recipients."

Belatedly, the policy discussion has moved in this direction—not simply how to get people into work, but how to get workers out of poverty. By now, we have a good idea of how to boost the prospect of low-income workers. First, they need generous support services that don't vanish when welfare expires—notably, health insurance and child care. At the state level, workers need healthy "earned-income disregards"—formulas that allow them to retain part of their benefits even as their paychecks grow (see Gordon L. Berlin, "Welfare That Works"). At the federal level, workers need an increase in the minimum wage and an expansion in the Earned Income Tax Credit (EITC) to help push more of them over the poverty line. Workers also need access to more training and education, to help them advance individually, and stronger unions, to help them advance collectively.

But in most of the country, officials are only beginning to think about things like wage progression and job retention. Few states have provided anything beyond the most rudimentary training courses.

Worse, many welfare leavers have been denied basic support services. Nationwide, more than a million people have lost their Medicaid. And only 10 to 15 percent of families eligible for federal child-care subsidies get them (see Jonathan Cohn, "Child's Play").

While some of this is due to ignorance or naïveté on the part of workers, much reflects the ongoing determination of welfare offices to save money (see Marcia Meyers, "How Welfare Offices Undermine Welfare Reform"). According to a recent study by the National Campaign for Jobs and Income, forty-five states are sitting on $7 billion in unspent Temporary Assistance for Needy Families (TANF) funds—money specifically earmarked by Washington to help ease the transition to work.

New York City exemplifies these trends. Under mayor Rudolph Giuliani, the city's welfare offices have been converted into job centers, but customers have been provided little beyond instruction in writing résumés and attending interviews. Those unable to find work in the private sector have been assigned "make work" jobs offering no prospect of advancement. Only in 2000, in his seventh year as mayor, did Giuliani get around to lining up job-placement agencies to help prepare people for work. But, characteristically, those agencies are all profit-making institutions, and the bidding process became bogged down in charges of nepotism and corruption.

Northern Light

Calling around again, amid all the gloomy reports, I did find a few bright spots. Wisconsin, draconian in other respects, had a good childcare program. Oregon was very conscientious about job placement. Vermont had no time limits for welfare aid (see Jon Margolis, "Vermont: The Greening of Welfare").

But the state I kept hearing about was Washington. Its governor, Gary Locke, is a Democrat whose Chinese-immigrant parents barely eked out a living running a restaurant and a grocery store—an experience that left him sensitive to the struggles of the working poor. From the start, Locke has talked about the importance of doing more than simply putting people to work. The motto of WorkFirst, as his program is called, is "a job, a better job, a career." WorkFirst, Locke has written, "is designed to give people the supports they need to get a job, learn new skills, and move up a career ladder so that they will be self-supporting for life. And WorkFirst is designed to offer the same supports to every low-wage worker who yearns for a better life—not just those who've been on the welfare rolls."

To help make that a reality, Locke has set up a special workforce subcabinet headed by his former budget director. Twice a month, the governor receives a report on caseload levels, wage averages, and job retention, and he is quick to intervene when the numbers go sour. To ensure maximum flexibility, Locke has secured the authority to allocate the money saved from caseload reduction as he sees fit, without having to receive the approval of the state legislature. In 2000, his administration spent $129 million on job placement and training—$100 million more than in 1997, when WorkFirst was introduced.

In another respect, too, Washington provides a good laboratory. Much has been written about the rise of the "new economy" and the gulf it has created between haves and have-nots, between those with master's degrees and software skills and those without. Few areas embody these trends more than Washington, especially the Seattle area. In the land of Microsoft, Amazon.com, and Boeing, the harsh realities of the global economy are on raw display, and I went to see what might be done to help its castoffs.

The Pioneer Square area of Seattle, where I stayed, is the city's oldest section, and now one of its most vital. Sandwiched between the waterfront and the downtown business district, it is filled with imposing redbrick buildings that, after a long period of neglect, have been restored to their turn-of-the-century elegance. Today, these buildings house art galleries, antique shops, design studios, high-tech start-ups, and, of course, hip coffee shops. Nearby is Safeco Field, the new home of the Seattle Mariners, and the majestic girders that span its roof seem to embody the city's soaring economic fortunes. The unemployment rate in Seattle is a meager 3.3 percent.

As plentiful as jobs are, though, many don't pay that well. In most downtown hotels, for instance, the housekeepers make about $6.50 an hour; sales clerks in the area's stores earn about $8 an hour. Across Lake Washington, in Redmond, the janitors at Microsoft start at $7.60 an hour. According to a "Job Gap" report published by the Northwest Policy Center at the University of Washington, the state's living wage, defined as the amount that allows a family to meet basic needs without resorting to public assistance, is $11.07 an hour for a single adult and $14.75 for a single adult with two children. According to the Northwest Policy Center, 37 percent of the jobs in the state pay less than the former and 73 percent pay less than the latter. The gap increases as welfare reform pushes more and more people into the workplace.

In its initial phase, welfare reform in Washington looked much as it does now in the rest of the country. The emphasis was on reducing caseloads, and no matter how many kids a mother had or how limited her job experience was, she was usually deemed fit to work. Referred to a job-search center, she would be put through a five-day workshop—concentrating on how to write a résumé—followed by an eleven-week search for a job. Beyond that, no training was provided, and clients were expected to take the first available job, no matter how dead-end it was.

In terms of getting people off welfare, WorkFirst was certainly successful: Between January 1997 and March 2000, the state's caseload dropped from 96,000 to 58,000, a 40 percent decline. In the Locke administration's first survey of leavers, the median wage of earners was $7.40 an hour, which was significantly higher than the state's minimum wage of $6.50 an hour. As the months passed, however, the median wage—far from increasing, as the state had anticipated—began slipping. The number of people returning to welfare also began rising, and that fed an increase in the overall caseload. To make matters worse, many families were routinely denied benefits to which they were entitled. In the most egregious case, 100,000 families were abruptly terminated from Medicaid, a result of the state's failure to reprogram its computers.

Seeing the gap between the governor's rhetoric and WorkFirst's actual performance, the state's poverty advocates began to mobilize. Washington's community-based groups are very vocal, and in the early days of WorkFirst, about seventy-five of them came together to form the Washington Welfare Reform Coalition. As the coalition became aware of the troubles families were having, it plotted ways to publicize them. At the end of WorkFirst's first year, for instance, as the state prepared to issue a rosy survey of how leavers had fared, the coalition released its own "Reality Check," highlighting the difficulties mothers were having paying the rent and feeding their kids. The press gave it ample coverage. "WorkFirst Gets Mixed Reviews in Early Years" ran a typical headline in the Tacoma *News Tribune.*

The Limits of Low-Wage Work

For a governor who had so forcefully stated his commitment to helping the working poor, such clips were embarrassing. But, to Locke's credit, he has responded. In late 1998, as WorkFirst was entering its second year, his administration began shifting the focus away from caseload reduction and toward poverty reduction. Though the program's policies are still evolving, Washington's experience since then provides a look at where other states and national policy could head in the future.

To begin, the state has sought to improve its delivery of support services. After long negotiations with the Welfare Reform Coalition, it has agreed to reinstate most of those who lost their Medicaid. It has also mounted media campaigns to publicize the availability of child care and to encourage workers to take advantage of the EITC. In addition, the state has set up a network of call centers to provide workers with information about benefit programs, tuition credits, and job referrals.

Washington's most creative efforts, however, have come in the area of job training. Community groups have been particularly outspoken on this point, arguing that low-income workers will never advance unless provided the opportunity to learn new skills. And the state has come to agree. Rather than insist that welfare recipients take the first available job, it now allows them to enroll in Pre-Employment Training (PET), an intensive twelve-week preparatory course. Offered at community colleges, PET provides instruction in "soft skills"—punctuality, grooming, workplace relations—as well as training in a specific field, like computers or bookkeeping. It's open not only to people on welfare but also to other workers who feel stuck in their jobs. And those with enough determination can take added instruction that will lead them up a career ladder to better-paying jobs (see Joan Fitzgerald and Virginia Carlson, "Ladders to a Better Life").

Can courses like PET make a difference? Sitting in on a PET class at Shoreline College, I was struck by the enthusiasm the students brought to it. "This part of WorkFirst is much better than when it first started," said a middle-aged woman with streaks of gray in her hair. "Before, you did a résumé, and that was it. Now, you're learning something."

"I could go get a job working at McDonald's," said another woman. "But I want to do better for myself." Having recently gotten a divorce after nineteen years of marriage, she said, she felt "sheer terror" at the prospect of entering the workforce, but the program was offering her some skills as well as the self-confidence she needed to go out and get a good job.

The early returns on the program have been encouraging; the average placement wage for graduates is $9.22 an hour, about $2 more than for WorkFirst clients not enrolled in PET. Yet, in a troubling sign, the wages have begun to decline as the enrollees grow more hard-core. "We're getting people with larger skills gaps and with multiple barriers to employment," said John Lederer, director of the program. Based on their preparation, Lederer said, these students could use up to twenty-six weeks of training. Unfortunately, state rules have limited them to twelve. Clearly, if PET is to have any effect, the state needs to be more flexible about its duration.

But Pre-Employment Training is just the beginning of sound policy, as I learned in an interview with Kay Hirai. One of Seattle's most visible, and unusual, entrepreneurs, Hirai owns Studio 904, an upscale hair salon with two sites, one of them in Pioneer Square. She also sits on the governor's Small Business Improvement Council. Over coffee, Hirai told me of her salon's unique no-tipping policy. Customers are charged a fee agreed upon in advance, and hair stylists receive a straight hourly wage (plus benefits). That wage begins at $8 to $9 an hour, but an employee can move up quickly to become a color specialist or business administrator and, after three years, can make close to $30,000.

Hirai is also unusual for her willingness to hire unskilled workers, including WorkFirst participants. "Let me tell you what it's like to hire a person from welfare," Hirai sighed. "The first six months are a big training time. You have to teach them so many things. And they have so many problems. They have problems with their children. They have problems getting to work on time. Eighty percent have English as a second language. And they are very angry because they have so much to deal with. So you have to do a lot of hand-holding."

Hirai recalls a twenty-three-year-old woman from Vietnam. She was good at cutting hair, but she had a child who demanded constant attention, and her English was very poor. Hirai hired her a personal tutor at $35 an hour. But it was all too much for the woman to juggle, and she eventually quit. Overall, of the fourteen welfare leavers that Hirai has hired and trained, only two have worked out. In some ways, she added, people not on welfare have it even harder because there are fewer supports available to them. Whether people are on welfare or off, she continued, "you have to keep training them." Short-term programs like PET are not enough, she said, adding, "There needs to be constant coaching. They need to be encouraged on a daily basis." The government, she went on, "needs to provide support for bringing these people along, and not just drop them off at the door."

Learning for the Long Term

Hirai's observations are borne out by the research on job training: Pre-employment courses, it shows, rarely produce lasting results. Training and guidance must continue long after the individual enters the workplace. Exactly how to provide this, though, has long eluded policy makers.

On a visit to Olympia, the Washington state capital, however, I found that the Locke administration is about to begin its own highly original experiment. Its mastermind is Ken Miller, the governor's policy adviser on welfare. A tough-minded, no-nonsense veteran of state government, Miller helped design WorkFirst, and he is, not surprisingly, a big booster of it. Nonetheless, he freely admitted to me that, during the program's first two years, "we had an extremely rigid system. It looked like we were trying to run the same type of narrow, mean-spirited program as in New York City, with success measured solely by caseloads going down."

As the number of people returning to welfare inched upward, Miller told me, the governor began pushing for changes. One was the introduction of PET. Quickly, however, it became clear that this was not enough, and so Miller and his team came up with a new idea: job coaches. In the program implemented in July 2000, each participant is assigned a coach to help her advance in the workplace. For each, a target wage is set, and training courses are arranged to help meet it. If the worker runs into problems at work, the coaches are there to intervene.

"We'll be trying to move people in the Puget Sound area to $11 to $13 an hour over three years," Miller said. The coaches are paid according to their success in moving clients toward that goal. The objective, Miller said, "is to ensure that everybody in the state has an opportunity to work in some fashion and move ahead as far as they can." The key, he added, "is to get people into job training while they're working." By February 2001, more than 1,500 participants had been assisted by coaches. The state initially allocated $10 million for the program, with participation limited to people who are, or have been, on welfare; eventually, though, it intends to open the program to all low-income workers.

As described by Miller, the job-coach idea seemed to me highly innovative—radical, even. Having not come across it in the welfare-to-work literature, I was eager to hear what others had to say about it. Most of the advocates and analysts I spoke with reacted positively. If the program actually succeeded in boosting workers' wages to the $11-to-$13 range, they said, it would be an impressive feat.

The main dissent, interestingly, came from a union leader. Marc Earls is the president of Local 6 of the Service Employees International Union (SEIU). Earls, a tall, poker-faced man with neatly cut sand-colored hair, quickly calculated that each coach would cost the state $50,000 a year in salary and benefits. An outlay of $10 million would translate into 200 coaches—a fraction of what was needed. "If the state hired the number really needed to get the job done," he observed, "job coaches would be the fastest-growing industry in the state." Workers, he added, "don't need coaches; they need unions."

Workers do, of course, need unions. The current resurgence of American labor, and the growing success of unions like the SEIU in organizing low-skilled workers, offer real hope for boosting living standards. But unionization is not a panacea. Seattle's janitors already are organized, yet they remain in poverty. Wages are kept down by the large pool of cheap labor in the area, fed by immigration and by welfare reform itself. Against this backdrop, any program that could raise workers' wages to $11 to $13 an hour would seem heaven-sent.

But is such a program practical? As Earls noted, hiring enough job coaches and providing all the training courses would be costly. And unless caseloads were kept very low, the whole venture would probably fizzle. But Ken Miller brushes aside such concerns. The state, he said, can draw on the $250 million it is saving every year in welfare expenditures, plus the $200 million it has accumulated in TANF funds. "What's limiting us right now isn't money, but how rapidly we can change our own culture and our systems," he noted. "If we can get two-year schools to create a curriculum and make it available to working families—a curriculum that business really wants to buy and that really helps working people get a better job—colleges would be flooded by the demand."

Even if the program is offered broadly, however, it would run into two other problems: the persistence of lots of low-wage jobs and the mismatch between available jobs seeking workers and the skills that low-wage workers currently possess. The former requires stronger unions and minimum-wage laws; the latter is addressed by another cutting-edge part of the Washington program—its emphasis on career ladders.

According to the Northwest Policy Center, there are 275,000 more households in the state of Washington than there are jobs that pay a living wage for a single adult, and at least one million more households than there are jobs that pay a living wage for a single adult with two children. "Despite strong economic growth in the regional economy," the center stated in a recent report, "the Northwest is not creating enough living wage jobs for all those who need them."

But at the same time, according to Mary Jean Ryan, director of

Seattle's Office of Economic Development, "there are labor shortages in all sectors, from Jack-in-the-the-Box to Microsoft." The most acute shortages, she said, are for mid-level jobs that require a two-year associate of arts degree in a technical field like infotech or biotech. "These are the jobs that companies are having the damnedest time recruiting for," she said. "The economy of thirty to fifty years ago was much more forgiving. You could go to high school and, if you had a reasonable work ethic, you could get a blue-collar job, work hard, and take care of what was needed. Right now, for a lot of people, that is not true." In the brave new world of the global marketplace, she added, "either you're on the road to prosperity or you're not, and the key is whether you have a good education and marketable skills. If you don't, you're not going to advance."

Ready for Prime Time?

Realistically, how many low-wage workers can be expected to gain such skills? In Seattle, I interviewed a number of low-income workers, and based on their backgrounds and abilities, they seemed to fall into three rough categories. A truly effective workforce policy would have to take these differences into account.

The first category—call them the Ready-for-Prime-Time Workers—is typified by José Deloisa, a janitor I met on a visit to the SEIU. An articulate forty-two-year-old Mexican with short, curly red hair and green eyes, José had worked for American Building Maintenance (ABM) for five years, cleaning the offices of high-tech companies. His pay came to $8.60 an hour, which produced a take-home check of $600 every two weeks—far short of what he needed to support his wife and three kids. Three years earlier, José told me, he had worked two part-time jobs in addition to his janitorial one, earning a combined $4,000 a month. But he was exhausted all the time, and his back eventually gave out. Now he was limited to light duty at ABM. After falling six months behind on rent, he and his family had been evicted from their apartment, and they were now living with friends, moving from one to another each month. To feed his family, he had to borrow money. On top of it all, ABM was trying to dismiss him.

Despite his dire situation, José refused to go on welfare or even to visit food banks—it was too demeaning, he felt. What he really wanted was more training. In Mexico he had attended college, studying mechanical engineering, but had dropped out due to a lack of funds. He had been very good at technical drawing, a skill much in demand in today's computer world. But José knows little about computers, and to learn more, he discovered, would cost between $6,000 and $10,000—a sum far beyond his means. "I can't stay as a janitor," he said plaintively. "I have the brains to do something else. But I need the training."

José represents that sector of the low-wage labor force that has a solid educational foundation but needs an additional year or two of training to advance. For most, the cost is beyond their reach, and since they're not on welfare, they do not qualify for government subsidies. If these workers had access to courses at community colleges, many would no doubt be able to fill the many semiskilled jobs that are going begging in today's economy. One possibility would be a working Americans education bill, modeled on the GI Bill, offering tuition credits or subsidies to every American who has been working for a minimum period of, say, two years, and whose annual income falls below, say, 200 percent of the federal poverty level.

A second group—the Eager Beavers—is personified by Shanndoah

Dowers, a forty-two-year-old mother of five living in north Seattle. Of Comanche, Cherokee, Eskimo, Irish, and Dutch heritage, Shanndoah dropped out of school after the ninth grade; after moving through a series of low-paying jobs, she ended up on welfare. Through WorkFirst, she enrolled in Pre-Employment Training at Shoreline Community College. During the week, Shanndoah works part time as an intern at the Welfare Rights Organizing Coalition in a community-service job subsidized by the state. It was there that I met her.

A cheery, strong-willed woman with dark eyes and full cheeks, Shanndoah has two of her children living with her. Just hearing her talk about her schedule left me exhausted. Every morning, she rises at 4:30 to get her youngest daughter (who is eight) ready for school. The school is on the opposite side of town, so they must board a bus at 7:00 in order to get there by 9:00. After dropping her daughter off, Shanndoah takes another bus into downtown Seattle, where she spends two hours paying bills, running errands, and doing homework. Then, at noon, she shows up at her job, where she remains for four hours. Then she hops on another bus to pick up her daughter, and together they take yet another bus home. There, she feeds her daughter, helps her with her homework, and does more of her own before turning in at 10:30. Her weekends are spent at Shoreline, where she's studying computers.

When WorkFirst was first introduced, Shanndoah said, "I thought, 'Oh my God, they want us off. We have no skills—what are we going to do?' " But her time at Shoreline has changed that. "I love the course and the high standards they set," she said. "Since I've been on the computer, I can't imagine doing anything else." When she finishes, Shanndoah expects to find a job paying $9 an hour. She thinks she needs $15 an hour to support her kids, however, and so, after getting settled in a job, she hopes to take advantage of another state program that will allow her to return to school part time. Through it, she hopes to get a GED and, eventually, a college degree.

Given her fierce determination, perhaps Shanndoah will be able to pull it all off. But with her limited education and responsibilities as a single mom, she will no doubt run into many problems. A job coach might be just the thing to help her cope—along with quality day care. Washington's new program will provide an important test of this approach's ability to help workers on this middle rung.

Finally, there is the Willing-but-Unable contingent, typified by Heather Madera. A twenty-six-year-old native of Rochester, New York, Heather dropped out of school in the twelfth grade and moved to Nevada, where she got involved with a man with whom she eventually had two children. After he became abusive, however, she moved with her eighteen-month-old daughter and three-month-old son to Washington, where her parents were living. There, she enrolled in WorkFirst. Heather's life, as she described it to me over the phone, seemed a chaotic patchwork of make-work jobs, long bus rides, day-care visits, apartment moves, and doctor's appointments for her children. At the time we spoke, she was suffering from strep throat and her son had an ear infection, and she was wondering how she would be able to afford medicine.

Heather told me she wanted to become a registered nurse. She struck me as bright and well motivated, and, in another world, perhaps she would be able to accomplish that goal. But the many obstacles she faces as a single mother of two would seem to make that unlikely. For people like her, even job coaches might not be enough help to achieve an acceptable living standard. Such hard-to-serve individuals will probably require various forms of government assistance over an extended period, including cash payments. In return, recipients can fairly be expected to perform some form of community service. One way or another, as the five-year time limits imposed by the 1996 act approach, states are going to have to consider creating some kind of rump system to deal with the sizable population that—no matter how many weeks of training they receive—will have a hard time making ends meet.

This, then, is what a manpower policy for the working poor might look like: a working American education bill for the top tier, job coaches and training for the middle, and a reconstituted (though much smaller) public-assistance system for the bottom. Needless to say, states will have to do a better job of providing parents with health care, child care, and the other support services they need.

Such a system will not come cheap, of course. But welfare reform has generated huge savings that can be invested in such initiatives. And the fact that these programs would help working Americans should make such expenditures politically palatable. As a result of welfare reform, politicians can no longer dismiss programs aimed at helping the poor on the grounds that recipients are lazy.

This will take political leadership. But the struggles of low-income workers have not gained much attention in the other Washington. Candidate Bill Clinton promised that if you worked hard and played by the rules, you wouldn't be poor. But President Clinton and a Republican Congress were more eager to "end welfare as we know it." When it came to welfare reform, the president seemed interested mainly in celebrating the reduction in caseloads. How to help the diligent working poor improve their lives did not fully engage him, nor has it moved the leadership of either of the two major political parties. With welfare reform, millions more Americans are playing by the rules, and most are still poor. With a full-employment economy and huge budget surpluses, they needn't be.

Holding Out

JOSHUA GREEN

One of the surest signs that a state has not fully committed to welfare reform is a large surplus of Temporary Assistance for Needy Families (TANF) funds. In Idaho, just $12 million of the $55 million received to date has been spent, yet the state has experienced an 89 percent drop in caseloads since August 1996 (2000 figures). This sharp caseload decline, coupled with low spending, is common to other Mountain West states like Wyoming and New Mexico.

Nationwide, $7 billion in TANF money remains unspent. The most common reason states invoke for holding on to money is the need for a rainy-day fund should caseloads suddenly increase. The healthy economy is another reason. Idaho officials point to the state's booming job market as one reason cash assistance has declined, which in turn lets the state conserve TANF money. But demographic data suggest other factors have contributed to the shrinking caseload. The number of cash recipients, for instance, dropped by more than half in a single month when the new welfare laws took effect on July 1, 1997. "We don't know definitely why so many people left," says Bill Walker, spokesman for the Idaho Health and Welfare Department. Antipoverty advocates say the reason was simple: When Idaho required everyone on Aid to Families with Dependent Children (AFDC) to reapply under the new program, huge numbers were simply turned away. Well-documented increases in demand at food banks and homeless shelters suggest that a decline in poverty hasn't matched the decline in caseloads.

Critics contend that Idaho isn't making a good-faith effort to reach out to the remaining poor. "Their feeling is that because they've been able to move folks off welfare, the program has been a success," said Kevin Borden, a campaign organizer for the Idaho Community Action Network. "But people are basically getting pushed off into minimum-wage jobs or further into poverty."

Idaho's welfare reserve and lingering poverty lend support to this assessment. There are any number of ways in which the state could reinforce welfare to work with its remaining TANF funds. Idaho ranks among the worst states in spending for children, education, and the poor. It has the shortest lifetime-eligibility period (two years) of any state and does not offer extensions or waivers to victims of domestic violence. When Idaho raised its maximum monthly payment, after years of pressure from groups like Borden's, it did so by only $14, to $293 a month. It is also the only remaining state in the country to count Social Security disability income in determining who qualifies for Medicaid, food stamps, or cash assistance. "The practical effect is that it eliminates families with disabled children in Idaho," said Wendell Primus, director of income security at the Center on Budget and Policy Priorities.

Poor families in every state have been losing Medicaid coverage and food stamps, both federal entitlements, when leaving welfare. This was not Congress's intent, but it is a side effect of many states' cost-cutting strategies. A 1999 report by congressional Republicans on the success of welfare reform agreed this was a problem that needed fixing.

Vermont: The Greening of Welfare

JON MARGOLIS

Before welfare reform, Jeannette, who has been getting benefits on and off since her marriage fell apart fifteen years ago, had never been sanctioned. Since then, it's happened every few months, and she's annoyed.

"First they sanctioned me in May [1999] for not meeting the fifteen-hour workweek requirement," she said. Being sanctioned meant she had to go to two meetings a month with welfare officials in St. Johnsbury, Vermont, and instead of getting her welfare check she got "vouchered." "I had to bring my bills over and they paid," she said.

Then, after she'd found herself more work, "they hassled me again because the minimum wage had gone up and I wasn't making enough money for it to count as fifteen hours. This time, we settled it by phone."

Actually, Jeannette (not her real name), who is about to turn fifty and lives with her youngest child in a mobile home on an unpaved road about halfway between St. Johnsbury and Montpelier, doesn't think she should have to get a job at all. She takes care of a disabled woman every weekend and an older person for a few hours during the week. She says that's enough.

"We have to get away from judging people simply by how much money they make," she said. "They tell me I should do something different, but I don't push paper well. I'm a people person. I'm not into telemarketing."

The telemarketing reference didn't come out of the blue. The state and federal governments are subsidizing a private company that will soon open a telemarketing center in Newport, near the Canadian border. DeeDee, a twenty-nine-year-old welfare mother who lives in Newport, would love to become a telemarketer and is also enthusiastically enrolled in a job-training program to improve her keyboard skills. She has no quarrel whatever with welfare reform. "I want to be self-supporting," said DeeDee (her real name, but the only one she'd give).

Jeannette and DeeDee come close to being at the poles of the national debate over welfare reform and whether it's working. Their stories also suggest what's unusual about Vermont. "In some states, welfare reform is about reducing the number of people on welfare," said Dan Bloom of Manpower Demonstration Research Corporation in New York, which evaluates welfare programs around the country. "Vermont's goal was to reduce people's sole reliance on welfare. In Vermont, a person who was mixing work and welfare was considered to have become less dependent." And that was counted a success.

Which is not to say that Vermont officials are indifferent to saving money. In fact, Vermont governor Howard Dean and his Social Welfare Department originally wanted to impose the "full-family sanctions" that most states have since adopted, terminating all benefits as punishment for repeated noncompliance with welfare-to-work rules. They were stymied by a small but very vocal and very tough pro–poor folks lobby.

That, too, illustrates a Vermont peculiarity: not the existence of advocates for the poor—lots of states have those—but the absence of any visible opposition to them. When Vermont's legislative committees deliberated over new welfare bills earlier this year, the most "conservative" voice in the room belonged to Social Welfare chief Sandy Dooley, the liberal Democratic appointee of a moderate Democratic governor. Her opponents were from the Vermont Low Income Advocacy Council and other allies of welfare. The Chamber of Commerce was not there fighting for deeper cuts.

Those lobbyists for the poor don't win all their battles in Vermont. But their clout may have been enough to convince state officials never even to propose the biggest stick of all available under the federal welfare reform law of 1996: the five-year lifetime limit on welfare benefits.

Vermont is not the only state that has decided not to impose the five-year limit or total-family sanctions. But it is one of the few, and it has attracted attention—admiring, skeptical, or just curious—from officials and policy mavens in other states. "We're trying a kinder, gentler approach to welfare reform," said state representative Paul Poirier, who chairs the House Committee on Health and Welfare.

In this effort, Vermont has several advantages, the first of which is that is started early and thus had considerable freedom to design its own course. Howard Dean was a New Democrat before anyone heard the term, and in 1994 Vermont became one of the first states to get a federal waiver to experiment with new rules designed to transform welfare recipients into employees.

Its rules were hardly draconian. There were no work requirements at all for 40 percent of those on welfare, and most of the others could wait more than two years before starting the "Reach-up" job-preparation program. But something must have worked, because the number of families on the rolls declined from 10,000 in 1994 to 6,200 in March 1999. While no one knows what happened to those 3,800 households (about 10,000 people), there is no evidence that they are worse off.

Another Vermont advantage: Dean, though a New Democrat, is a Democrat, and a physician and a devotee of universal health insurance, which he has come very close to achieving in his state. More than 90 percent of Vermont youngsters are covered under a program known as "Dr. Dinosaur," and the low-income mothers of those children are covered, too, even if they're working. This all but eliminates one of the burdens of welfare reform; you don't lose your health benefits when you go off the rolls.

It is also relatively easy to take the kinder, gentler approach in a small, homogenous state where kind and gentle are practically a tradition. Indeed, Vermont's political culture sometimes threatens to degenerate into cloying and treacly. Still, there is something to be said for civility, and state officials are serious about it, as they recently demonstrated in the generally civilized debate over gay and lesbian partnerships. To take just one oddity: Representative Poirier is a Democrat, which is unsurprising for a committee chair in a legislative body with a Democratic majority. But his Senate counterpart, Health and Welfare Committee chair Helen Riehle, is a Republican, though the Democrats run that house, too.

In Vermont, this is no big deal. It isn't that there's no partisanship. It's just that partisanship is restrained. This may be the only state in which the center aisles do not divide the parties in the legislative chambers: Senators sit by county, and House members draw their seats by lot. It's harder to get bitterly angry at the person sitting next to you every day.

Legislators, of course, reflect their constituents, and while antipathy to welfare recipients is hardly absent in Vermont, it does seem milder than in most other states, for two obvious reasons. In many states the welfare population is concentrated in a city or two, making it easy for the suburban majority to scorn recipients as vaguely alien. Vermont doesn't have a suburban majority, at least not yet, and a woman on welfare is more likely to live in a double-wide on an unpaved road than in a city slum.

And she's more likely to look like her employed neighbors. In Vermont, the racial complication that bedevils the welfare debate nationally is all but absent, simply because nonwhites are all but absent. They were 1 percent of the population in 1990; they might be 2 percent now. The welfare population is 95 percent white. There is no way to quantify how much this softens antiwelfare sentiments. There is no way to deny that it does.

But if Vermont's right wing has been quiet in the welfare debate, the state's welfare approach is still a victory of sorts for conservatives. There is, for one thing, a limit to how sharply any state can deviate from the new federal rules, and Vermont has already tightened some of its own. That fifteen-hour work requirement that Jeannette failed to meet is about to become twenty hours (still lower than the federal recommendation of thirty hours). And any mother whose youngest child is six or older will have to enter the work-preparation "Reach-up" program immediately and actively seek employment after one year.

"Our welfare reform is less onerous, but it does represent a major watershed in policy," said Sandy Dooley. "It imposes a work requirement on single parents."

Even on Jeannette, who avoided another sanction recently by getting a part-time job with the Census Bureau. But then she was late in reporting the income and was told she would get no benefits in May. The Census job would be gone by then, so she faced the prospect of living through the month on only her $624 earned income, without the $500 or so she has been getting from welfare.

She'll work it out one way or another. She's resourceful, and stubborn, too. For instance, she gets no rent subsidy because the wood stove that heats her mobile home doesn't meet safety standards, but she won't move. She likes where she lives, and she likes her wood stove.

DeeDee gets the rent subsidy and the job training. And she'll take that telemarketing job as soon as it's available. She isn't as sophisticated as Jeannette, but she does understand the futility of continuing to argue about whether she's obligated to support herself. Even in Vermont, that debate is over.

The Welfare Shell Game

JOSHUA GREEN

At first glance, it hardly seems noteworthy—a handful of foster-care programs in Texas were paid for last year with money from the state's $600 million federal welfare surplus instead of with state funds, as they are traditionally. But the $162 million Texas had ear-marked for the foster-care programs was instead added to the state's general fund, where it helped finance a tax cut from the state's $6.4 billion surplus. While the Temporary Assistance for Needy Families (TANF) money might have gone to a worthy cause, it didn't help those for whom it was intended: the welfare poor.

By substituting federal funds for state funds, states like Texas, flush with large TANF surpluses as a result of declining caseloads, have essentially laundered federal welfare dollars to finance more politically popular programs. New York alone diverted more than $1 billion.

Because a provision in the 1996 federal welfare law allows states to spend TANF money on any program that received federal money under TANF's predecessor, Aid to Families with Dependent Children (AFDC), there is nothing illegal about substituting federal welfare dollars for state dollars. So states like Texas can free up state funds by plowing large amounts of TANF money into social services like foster care that, in fact, received scant federal funding under AFDC. But doing so denies the poor supplemental programs that progressive states have created with surplus money to help people leave welfare—programs like child care, job training, or larger cash grants (Texas still ranks forty-seventh in the size of its maximum monthly payment to a family of three).

It also threatens future TANF funding for all states. "It's a risky practice because whatever savings states generate could disappear when Congress reassesses the size of state grants," said Ed Lazere, a policy analyst for the Center on Budget and Policy Priorities, who specializes in state assistance programs.

In March, Connecticut Republican Nancy Johnson, who chairs the House subcommittee overseeing welfare reserve funds, fired the opening salvo in what advocates for the poor fear is an effort to scale back state grants. "It would be a shame if a few states . . . replaced state dollars with TANF dollars in order to provide tax cuts, build roads or bridges, or in general use funds for non-TANF purposes," Johnson warned in a letter to state governors. "These jurisdictions could provoke Congress to take actions that would hold serious consequences for every state."

There is not yet a reliable measure of how many states engage in this type of budgetary switch or how much TANF money has been diverted. But congressional Republicans hoping to slash state welfare grants will have a potentially damaging weapon in hand when reauthorization comes up in two years. The General Accounting Office has begun an investigation to determine the size and scope of the practice and hopes to report its findings early next year.

Tough Sanctions, Tough Luck

JOSHUA GREEN

Like many states that aggressively enforce welfare laws, South Carolina has seen its caseload plummet. But much of the state's success results from its perverse sanctions policy. South Carolina is one of fourteen states that mandates that a single instance of noncompliance result in a loss of benefits for the entire family, including children.

According to Sue Berkowitz, director of the South Carolina Appleseed Legal Justice Center, clients have been sanctioned because they couldn't find transportation to work or were tardy for class. Recently, a single mother was sanctioned for being late to an appointment with a caseworker because she was visiting her daughter in the hospital. In a rare appeal, the mother prevailed and the sanction was lifted, only to be imposed again a month later when her bus broke down and she was late to work.

If a mother twice provides the state with incorrect information about a child's father—even one with whom she's been out of contact for a decade—she is banned for life from receiving welfare. "With felony enforcement, it's three strikes and you're out," says Berkowitz. "If a woman can't give proper information on the dad, it's two strikes and you're out."

It is a system designed to frustrate and discourage applicants. A 1999 study by the Heritage Foundation found—the usual conservative storyline notwithstanding—that the nationwide decline in caseload was almost entirely due to tough state sanction policies and that the robust economy and low unemployment rate had little effect. States like South Carolina, which imposed immediate full-check sanctions, saw a staggering 42 percent drop in caseloads, while states with progressively more severe sanctions dropped 28 percent. Those that Heritage considered "weak" sanction states (they only docked the "adult" portion of the TANF check) dropped just 17 percent, thus confirming what anti-poverty advocates have long argued: Sanctions encourage people to give up. So declining caseloads do not necessarily reflect declining need.

On the contrary, sanctions punish those least equipped to handle them. According to a recent General Accounting Office report, studies of families under sanction indicate that they have lower education levels and less work experience than the TANF population in general. Consequently, once welfare payments stop, they rely more heavily on support from family and friends than from employment income. Sanctions alienate the most needy recipients while creating an adversarial climate that discourages those who might benefit from help. Indeed, the biggest challenge for South Carolina social-service organizations has not been to appeal sanctions but to convince people who qualify for benefits to apply in spite of the draconian atmosphere. Mothers who go into the program, for instance, can qualify for two years of Medicaid and two years of child care, even if they go off welfare a month later.

Tough sanctions are an all-too-effective and politically popular method of purging welfare rolls, but one that operates in fundamental opposition to welfare reform's stated goal of getting the poor back to work. Jim Hodges, South Carolina's Democratic governor, has promised a more moderate approach, but it has only begun to trickle down to welfare offices.

How Welfare Offices Undermine Welfare Reform

The Fine Art of Dissuading People from Collecting Benefits

MARCIA K. MEYERS

Welfare and related policy reforms adopted by Congress in the 1990s seemed to strike an implicit bargain with low-wage working families. Parents were expected to meet their "personal responsibility" for supporting themselves and their children by leaving welfare and going to work. If they did, government would help out by providing a package of income, health insurance, and child-care assistance to "make work pay," even for low earners. Four years out, there is disquieting evidence that government is not keeping its side of the bargain—largely because we have failed to develop the appropriate administrative systems and capacity to deliver assistance to the working poor. This ostensibly bureaucratic failure happens to serve the goal of many elected officials to avoid spending money on the poor. But if our commitment to "end welfare as we know it" without impoverishing families is genuine, these administrative problems must be addressed.

To understand why low-income working families are failing to get or keep the supportive assistance that was designed to help them achieve self-sufficiency, one needs to look beyond legislated policies to examine the details of program delivery. This is work that several colleagues and I are pursuing in our research on child care and welfare reform at the state and local levels—talking to program managers and staff, studying program operations, and observing the experience of program applicants and clients as they negotiate the system. What we have observed is disturbing: The state and local welfare systems that distribute support services to poor individuals remain ill equipped to serve a new population of working poor families.

Let me say up front that I am a sympathetic observer of welfare programs. I have worked in, managed, and studied these programs for many years. I believe them to be staffed by diligent individuals who want to do a good job. I have also observed widespread support, at the agency and staff levels, for efforts to move welfare toward a system that rewards and supports work. What I have not seen is a reformulation of the systems, administrative structures, and incentives to allow welfare offices to do a good job in keeping the government side of the welfare reform bargain.

One can glean particularly revealing insights by considering the organization of several kinds of help for low-income individuals: help accessing the system, help understanding what benefits are available, help finding the services they need, and help keeping the benefits for which they are eligible.

Getting the Word Out

The first form of help that low-income individuals need is information. Learning about the benefits for which they may be eligible turns out to be a surprisingly difficult hurdle for many. Although low-income individuals are often portrayed as knowledgeable and savvy consumers of welfare services, more systematic research reveals that their information is often both limited and inaccurate.

Child care may be one of the most important, but least well-known, benefits available to low-income parents. In a 1995 survey of current and former welfare recipients in California, for example, my colleagues and I found that two-thirds to three-quarters of mothers did not know about employment-related child-care subsidies. More recent studies in Florida, Massachusetts, and South Carolina reveal that, even in the wake of welfare reforms, 40 to 60 percent of former welfare recipients remain unaware of child-care assistance for which they may be eligible. Given that recipients exiting the welfare system have been the primary target of new child-care subsidy programs, knowledge is likely to be even lower among low-earning families who have had little contact with the welfare system.

Similarly, a recent study of food stamp participation found that 60 percent of families who were poor enough, but not receiving food stamps, had never applied for assistance because they did not know they were eligible. Notably, only 13 percent indicated that they failed to apply because they didn't need help.

Though local welfare offices now routinely call their clients "customers," they have had little practice drumming up business. Welfare program operations are designed, first and foremost, to sort applicants into two groups, those who are eligible for benefits and those who are not, and then to serve the subset determined eligible. Until the recent decline in welfare caseloads, the demand for assistance exceeded staff and other organizational resources. (Many programs still face the same constraints because they have been downsized as caseloads have dropped.) Given that their workload increases directly with the number of applicants they must process and serve, welfare administrators and staff have had little reason to beat the bushes for more applicants. Indeed, given the persistent and growing public pressure to reduce caseloads, they have had distinct disincentives to seek out additional customers.

(It is noteworthy that staff and administrators in these programs usually define their work as starting once an individual arrives at the office to apply for benefits. One of the most revealing questions I ask local welfare administrators is: What share of the area's poor population do you serve? This is a question that few have been able to answer because the "customers" they collect data on are welfare recipients rather than poor people.)

So it should not be surprising to learn that welfare programs have done little or no outreach to advertise welfare benefits, and that this pattern has carried over to the provision of nonwelfare support services. Local welfare administrators and staff tell us they assume that low-income families "already know" about child-care benefits through informal information channels, or that they have been given the information by another agency—one that specializes in employment support or child care.

Yet outreach efforts of other public agencies are also minimal. Staff at many community-level child-care agencies, for example, think outreach is unnecessary because funds are limited and families are already on waiting lists. Other staff are afraid that active outreach will create a demand for services that cannot be met. The result, as the survey data suggest, is that many families who may be eligible for assistance never hear about it or receive inaccurate information through informal channels.

Helping Individuals Access the System

Unfortunately, those who know enough to seek benefits may face even more formidable hurdles when they encounter the welfare office. In some communities, there are now alternative entry points for the working poor to obtain nonwelfare assistance: Individuals may sign up for Medicaid at a local health clinic or for child-care benefits through a child-care resource and referral program. But for most individuals, and for any who hope to qualify for food stamps, the point of entry is still the local welfare office. (In fact, many areas still use a single application for all three programs, a by-product of earlier reforms designed to simplify the application process.) Once again, the welfare system turns out to be poorly equipped to help them.

The administrators and staff of welfare programs, like those in any public organization, try to be responsive to the expectations of the public and of elected political officials. Over a period of many years, these administrators and staff perfected procedures for doing what was expected of them: sorting eligible from ineligible applicants, detecting fraudulent claims, and generally discouraging demand for welfare services. As the entry point for supportive assistance to the working poor, welfare programs are now expected to play a more nuanced role—as one local administrator described it, to treat reliance on government for welfare as "bad" but "Medicaid as not so bad" and "child care as good."

Welfare programs are not only poorly equipped for this more nuanced task, but in many communities they are moving in directions that will aggravate the problem. Applying for welfare is, by design, an arduous, time-consuming, and generally unpleasant process. It also exposes individuals to eligibility determination procedures that are more localized, less uniform, and often more arbitrarily applied than those of unstigmatized government programs (such as Social Security). The welfare rights movement of the 1970s forced local welfare systems to operate with greater uniformity and due-process protections for clients. With the welfare reforms of the 1990s, Congress reversed this nascent trend toward uniformity by devolving control over welfare eligibility rules and procedures to the states. In their zeal to reduce welfare caseloads and costs, many states have used this new authority to impose more complex eligibility tests for welfare. As a result, in many parts of the country, getting welfare has become even more difficult and unpleasant than it used to be. And the welfare office, with its difficult processes, is the system that many low-income workers have to go through to find out if they are eligible for other forms of assistance.

In one county in the Northeast, for example, welfare applicants must now complete up to six different in-person appointments in order to be approved. These appointments include an intake interview with a welfare examiner, an orientation and assessment at the local Department of Labor, an interview with a child-support enforcement official, and—at the discretion of the welfare examiner—a drug and alcohol screening at the Health Department and an office appointment and home visit by a fraud investigator. For each of these required appointments, the applicant is obligated to collect a different set of documents to verify her financial and personal circumstances—typically birth certificates, school records, proof of residence from the landlord, additional proof of residence from a "professional person," wage and bank records, and a written statement from her past employer certifying that she has indeed been terminated. In some circumstances, even more documents may be required—such as car registrations, statements from absent parents about the amount of child support they contribute, divorce papers, and even funeral programs (in cases of recent widowhood).

As the applicant is visiting schools, landlords, neighbors, ex-employers, and others to collect her verification, she may be required to attend job-search programs or to document her independent job-search activities; she may be enrolled in mandatory drug or alcohol treatment; she may undergo a full investigation by the fraud unit. If she fails to follow through on any of these steps, her application will be "closed" without a formal determination of eligibility.

Not surprisingly, a large number of this county's applications are "closed" before they are completed. (With six mandatory appointments, even if applicants had a 90 percent probability of keeping each appointment and bringing in all the required paperwork, their probability of making it through the entire process would be barely 50 percent.) Because welfare staff do not keep records on this, they know little or nothing about what happens to most applicants who don't make it through the county's rigorous eligibility tests. Most unsuccessful applicants just disappear. Whether they disappear because they find work and decide to forgo benefits, or because they are overwhelmed and discouraged by the process, is anyone's guess. How many were potentially eligible for other, nonwelfare assistance is an even greater mystery.

While the details vary from place to place, the system in this county is not particularly unusual. The elaboration of eligibility processes reflects both federal and state priorities. The federal welfare reforms require states to involve welfare recipients in employment-related activities, and many states have added on other up-front requirements, ranging from drug screening to parenting classes. Most states have also retained or even enhanced their procedures for error and fraud detection. (They have done this with good reason. While the welfare reforms relaxed federal oversight of welfare determinations, the Department of Agriculture still imposes penalties for "quality control" errors in food stamps.)

From the perspective of welfare system administrators, tough fraud detection and aggressive diversion of applicants are among the chief successes of welfare reform precisely because they have contributed to the remarkable decline in caseloads. But the largely unnoted consequence is the diversion of low-income individuals from the nonwelfare supportive services they may need to achieve self-sufficiency on low wages. It is difficult to estimate how many are affected because welfare systems rarely track these "noncases." However, a declining food stamps caseload and lower than expected participation in new child health and child-care programs suggest that the number may be large.

Helping Applicants Find the Right Services

Even if an applicant manages to make it into and through the arduous system of welfare application, her chances of getting the right information, referrals, and applications for supportive assistance remain uncertain. The rules governing entry to Medicaid have grown more complex over the years, as policies have changed, new rules have been adopted, and court decisions have codified rights for sometimes very narrowly defined groups. In many states, child care continues to be nearly as complicated, with separate rules for those in welfare, leaving welfare, or outside the welfare system. In order to obtain these benefits, applicants need information, assistance, and often the time and goodwill of the workers who make eligibility determinations. Frontline workers, in turn, need both a detailed knowledge of the system and time to determine claimants' needs and match them to the right services. Unfortunately, many welfare workers have neither—even when they have plenty of goodwill.

Two examples from visits to local welfare offices illustrate how easy it can be for a claimant to narrowly miss out on assistance for which she may be eligible. In one welfare office encounter in a southeastern state, a single mother of two began the multistep process of qualifying for welfare by telling an eligibility screener that she needed help: She was about to be evicted from her home because she was under treatment for depression, out of work, and behind on her mortgage payments. Because the screener was intent on doing her job—which was to sort the applicant into the right sequence of employment-preparation activities—she didn't have the time or expertise to address the housing problem. The best she could do was to suggest that the woman let herself be evicted and move to a homeless shelter in order to move up on the priority list for public housing. By the end of the morning, the applicant had been assessed for employment and sent off to job-search training, but no one had directed her across the office to the emergency assistance staff.

In another encounter, this time in a southwestern state, a recently unemployed mother came to her meeting with the welfare examiner with what she hoped was the right paperwork to apply for welfare, food stamps, and Medicaid. She met with an experienced but harried welfare worker who was trying to master a new computerized intake system. Over the course of the next two hours, she answered questions about her family (Social Security numbers, places of birth, mothers' maiden names), about her own and her husband's employment (prior work, reasons for leaving, self-employment income), and about her car (it had broken down) and other assets (she had none). She was required to sign a Personal Responsibility Agreement and to call her landlord so that the worker could verify that her son did in fact live with her. She was directed to get her child's immunization records, to apply for unemployment insurance, to obtain bank statements, to bring in utility bills, to attend a parenting class and a work orientation session, and to have her husband document his self-employment expenses and get a letter of termination from his last employer. But in the end, she could not pursue her application for cash assistance because she could not produce her birth certificate. She settled for opening a food stamp application (for which she did not need the birth certificate) and left the office—late for a scheduled job interview.

Throughout the more than two-hour encounter, she was told to do many things. She signed many forms. But she was not told about the availability of assistance to help her make ends meet once she returned to work. She was never told that she would probably be eligible for low-income Medicaid even if she found a job (although she complained that her last job "didn't provide medical"). She was never told that she might qualify for child-care benefits (even though her son was not yet in school). She was not counseled about the Earned Income Tax Credit (EITC) or about employment or training services. If she was lucky enough to get the job she interviewed for that afternoon, she was likely to earn too much to keep her food stamps and unlikely to connect with any assistance that would help her support her family on low wages.

In many if not most states, the administrative structure and capacity of the welfare system are still similarly at odds with the job of helping low-income individuals obtain supportive services. Even when they have the potential "customer" in hand, frontline welfare workers are often too busy or too preoccupied with eligibility concerns to do much in the way of counseling applicants.

Helping Clients Keep Benefits

In many programs, it is nearly as hard to retain benefits as to obtain them. In studying the duration of child-care assistance in a number of states, for example, we have found that children generally receive subsidies for only a few months. The reasons they leave the system are likely to be varied—parents may lose their jobs, change their schedules, lose their child-care providers, or decide to go without assistance. But the complexity of keeping a child-care subsidy appears to contribute to these exits as well. As in other areas of assistance to the working poor, welfare systems turn out to be better equipped to avoid processing errors that cost the state money than they are to help working families meet their needs.

Consider the system in one northeastern state. As a parent moves into, through, and out of the welfare system, she will probably interact with three separate agencies in order to qualify for child-care assistance: a workfare agency (when she is receiving TANF and participating in a mandatory work-experience activity), a welfare office (when she has earnings but is still receiving TANF), and a transitional services office (when she earns enough to become ineligible for TANF). In each system, she is required to make an initial application in person and to recertify her eligibility in person every six months. Each month she receives child-care assistance, she will need to have the child-care provider fill out a voucher certifying services and send the voucher to the relevant welfare agency; she will also need to comply with whatever the welfare system requires of her (for example, showing up for her work-experience activity) and submit pay stubs documenting her earnings. If her paperwork is all in order, the welfare agency will then issue her a check to pay the child-care provider.

This is the routine if all goes well. But it is easy for things to go badly. Her child-care payment may be delayed by agency paperwork problems. Her child-care case will be closed if she is determined to be noncompliant with some aspect of the welfare program and is sanctioned. Her case may close, even if she is compliant, if her welfare status changes, if the paperwork goes awry during the transition from one child-care system to the next, or if the agency makes a coding error.

Given the complexity of the administrative and information-management systems involved, it is not surprising that these errors are common. What should be surprising, and disturbing, is the extent to which the cost of the errors falls on the parent rather than the state. The child-care subsidy system in many counties is biased in the direction of saving the state money. When the eligibility status of a child-care case is in doubt, the usual system response is to avoid a potential overpayment by withholding benefits. For the welfare administrator who has to balance the books, this approach is fiscally sound. But for the working parent who has already incurred a child-care bill, or for the caregiver who has already provided services, this approach may be financially disastrous.

When lawmakers in Congress and state legislatures set out to "reform" welfare, they started with the obvious targets. They restricted access to welfare and liberalized spending for supportive services designed to serve as a transition from welfare reliance to welfare independence. The reform was incomplete, however, because they left the delivery of these support services to a welfare system that has neither the incentives nor the organizational capacity to advertise and deliver them. As a result, many working families are not getting the help they need to achieve self-sufficiency on low wages. This is not inconsistent with the reluctance of many elected officials to spend money on the poor. But it is also not inevitable. Rather, it means that lawmakers committed to real reform of the system will need to consider changes not only in the rules and regulations, but in the delivery system as well. Fortunately, there are examples, in the United States and abroad, of alternative approaches.

In terms of getting the word out, there is good reason to believe that, with the proper incentives and resources, public agencies can do effective outreach and case-finding. One of the most impressive recent examples is the children's Supplemental Security Income (SSI) program. In a 1990 ruling in *Sullivan v. Zebley,* the Supreme Court liberalized the criteria used for determining children's eligibility for disability benefits. In order to apply the new rules fairly, the Social Security Administration directed its regional field offices to conduct outreach in order to identify newly eligible children and those who were denied benefits under the earlier rules. Importantly, this directive was funded. The SSI program was also an uncapped entitlement for qualifying children, and finding cases had financial benefits for state and local welfare agencies (because shifting poor children from welfare to the fully federal SSI program saved state and local governments matching funds). Within a few years, many local welfare agencies had staff specifically assigned to the task of finding potentially eligible children and helping them qualify for benefits. The results were impressive. In the four years following the *Zebley* ruling, with aggressive outreach by Social Security and welfare offices, the number of child cases in the SSI program tripled. (The increase was so dramatic, in fact, that children's SSI benefits were later targeted for cutbacks in the 1996 welfare reform bill.)

Getting the word out about supportive benefits is an important first step. But it is only the first step. If lawmakers want working poor families, who are often as short of time as they are of money, to access these benefits, they will also need to make the delivery system more "user friendly."

Some state and local welfare systems have taken steps in this direction. One approach has been to consolidate welfare, child care, and employment services and to expand the authority and skills of frontline workers. States are experimenting with "seamless" systems of child-care funding to minimize the difficulty of retaining benefits over time. Others are developing new approaches to inform parents about child health insurance benefits—from hotlines to community-based intake systems.

Many states and localities are moving some portion of support services out of the welfare system and into alternative government agencies or community-based organizations. This decentralization and privatization of services may help working families access assistance by separating it from the restrictive and hostile systems that dominate welfare offices.

Decentralization and privatization may have advantages, but they may also have important limitations. Decentralization can backfire if it creates more complex and fragmented systems that increase transaction costs for potential applicants. Private agencies, no matter how user-friendly, are also constrained by the funding and rules of the programs they deliver. Many private child-care resource and referral programs, for example, report that they would like to expand their scope of service, but they are implicitly or explicitly discouraged from doing so due to shortages of child-care funding. Finally, the private sector has plenty of its own "bad seeds"—agencies that abuse government funds and even clients. Given the inherent difficulty of monitoring the activities of nongovernmental organizations, a cautious approach to widespread privatization may be warranted.

A more fruitful approach may be to consider the public systems that work well for the delivery of other forms of government assistance. The tax system, for example, now delivers cash assistance through the EITC to millions of low-income families, though these benefits are still provided in a single lump sum at tax time, which does little to help struggling families meet their ongoing work and other expenses. Social Security provides an even more encouraging example. Because the emphasis is on getting benefits out rather than keeping applicants out, the Social Security Administration operates with exemplary efficiency to provide assistance to millions of recipients and spends only an estimated 1 percent of its funds on administration.

To find other models for delivery of government services, it helps to look farther afield and consider models developed in the industrialized countries of Western Europe. Cash assistance for families is well established in most of these countries in the form of child allowances (which may be means-tested or taxable in order to target benefits on lower-income families). An even more encouraging example can be found in the delivery of child-care services. In most of these countries, more than 80 percent of children attend publicly supported child care by their third birthday, and nearly all low-income working parents have access to public child care when their children are even younger. These services have grown substantially over the past two decades, easily weathering recent, much-heralded retrenchments in several of the European welfare states. Widespread support for such services suggests that an active government role in providing assistance to working families is both politically and operationally feasible, given the right administrative structures.

In the United States, many disadvantaged parents are keeping their side of the welfare bargain, especially single mothers, who constitute the large majority of welfare recipients. Whether they have been pushed by more demanding welfare rules or pulled by a tight labor market, the number of single mothers receiving welfare has plummeted since 1996, while the number employed has increased at a remarkable rate.

On one level, government appears to have kept its side of the bargain as well. Congress expanded the EITC in the early 1990s and raised the minimum wage in 1996. Federal and state governments are also spending more on child-care assistance. Congress has authorized new federal funds with a more generous matching rate to encourage states to expand health coverage for poor children. Considered together, these policies form a reasonably generous alternative safety net for working but low-earning families. The Council of Economic Advisers says that, with the EITC, a parent with two children who works full time for the minimum wage can now have income above the poverty line. If she and her children are covered by government health insurance, and if she has subsidies to cover her child-care expenses, she has a reasonable chance to achieve self-sufficiency.

However, the operative word in this optimistic scenario is "if." Families can hope to achieve self-sufficiency on low wages *if* they receive the extra income from the EITC and food stamps, *if* they have health insurance, and *if* they receive child-care subsidies. To date, the evidence suggests that far too many working but poor families are not receiving this package of assistance: Food stamp caseloads are declining at an unprecedented rate, and, according to researchers at the Urban Institute, about two-thirds of families leaving food stamps appear to be still poor enough to qualify for assistance. Analysts at the Urban Institute have also found that as many as three-quarters of low-income children without health insurance seem to live in families whose income is low enough to have qualified them for it. And despite substantial new child-care spending, only 10 to 14 percent of eligible families appear to be served by the major federal child-care program, the Child Care and Development Block Grant.

Much of the problem appears to lie not in legislative policy but in the structure and operation of state and local welfare systems that control outreach and intake for these programs. Given the historical role of the welfare system, this is not very surprising. Systems that work well to keep people out of welfare work poorly to get people into food stamps, health insurance, and child-care services.

As we move from narrowly targeted, tightly rationed "welfare" to more universal and readily accessible forms of assistance, a change in delivery systems is critical. This may represent an even more radical reform of the welfare system than that envisioned by Congress in 1996. But as the perennial question of "what to do about welfare" shifts from the problem of welfare reliance to the problem of continued economic insecurity for low earners, an equally radical shift in the answer is needed.

Leave No Child Behind?

The Inconsistent, Inefficient, and Unfair Way
We Support—and Fail to Support—Our Kids

NANCY FOLBRE

If there's one thing most Americans agree on, it is the ideal of giving all children a fair opportunity to succeed in life. Government programs such as Head Start and election-year slogans such as "Leave no child behind" invoke the time-honored metaphor of a contest that every child has a chance to win. The very idea of free public schooling is based on this goal—and to the extent that schools don't succeed in providing equal opportunity, they are vulnerable to criticism from liberals and conservatives alike.

But we're a long way from the "opportunity society" that our Horatio Alger–style political rhetoric extols. What we have is an "inequality society." The average income of the richest 20 percent of American families, for example, amounts to about twelve times the average of those in the bottom 20 percent. Families at the bottom spend more than they bring in, accumulating debt. Families at the top spend a lower percentage of their income, saving money and accumulating wealth. Economists estimate that most families spend about the same percentage of their total expenditures on their children. The end result is that at least five times as much private capital gets invested in kids at the top of the income spectrum as in those at the bottom.

Government is supposed to help level the playing field; as a practical matter, this requires providing more assistance to poor children than to rich ones. But public spending does little to counterbalance inequality. Overall, children in poor families receive only slightly more public support than children in rich ones, with families in the middle receiving significantly less than those at either end. But if one looks just at education, government support tends to benefit the affluent more than the poor. And our social safety nets for children provide more generous benefits to those who lose a parent through death than to those who lose one through desertion. Our system of public support for children is inconsistent, inefficient, and unfair.

Benefits for Rich and Poor

Most European countries provide support for children through a family allowance system in which parents receive a regular check in the mail. The United States tries to accomplish something similar through tax deductions and credits. The complexity of our tax system, however, means that different families get different amounts per child. And few citizens—indeed, few policy makers—really understand who gets what.

Let's take a look at how families with children are treated at different income levels. Those with income below the poverty level don't owe income taxes. Instead, low-income workers can take advantage of the

Earned Income Tax Credit (EITC), which gives them a "refund" from the IRS greater than the taxes that were withheld from their pay. This benefit applies to families in which one or both parents are earning income; the levels increase sharply for families with one child and again (less sharply) for families with two. No additional benefits are provided for families with three or more children. In 1999 a family with two children eligible for the maximum EITC would have received $3,816.

Families who earn enough income to owe federal taxes can subtract from their taxable income an exemption for every dependent. In 1999 this exemption was set at $2,750. By subtracting that amount, families in the 15-percent tax bracket would save about $412 a year. The same exemption would save families in the 31-percent tax bracket (with adjusted gross income between $104,050 and $158,550 for a married couple filing jointly) more than twice as much—$852. In addition to the exemption, families can deduct a $500 credit per child from their taxes. Thus, the overall benefit for a family in the 31-percent tax bracket with two kids is $2,704. That's less than the maximum EITC. But a high-income family with three kids would save $4,056, a more generous benefit than a family with three kids would receive from the EITC.

Here's the kicker: Tax benefits linked to child rearing follow a U-shaped pattern; they are highest at both ends of income distribution and lowest in the middle. Thus, a family in the 15-percent tax bracket with two children that is not eligible for the EITC enjoys a tax benefit of only $1,824.

Furthermore, relatively few families receive the maximum EITC because it phases out quickly as a family earns more than about $13,000 a year. This phaseout has the same effect as a higher tax rate for working families in the lower-middle part of the income distribution. Such inequity has prompted some policy makers to argue that eligibility for the

EITC should be expanded in a way that increases public support for child rearing among near-poor and middle-income families. David Ellwood and Jeffrey Liebman of the Kennedy School of Government at Harvard University advocate this approach. Robert Cherry of Brooklyn College at the CUNY Graduate Center and Max Sawicky of the Economic Policy Institute have developed a detailed proposal for a Universal Unified Child Credit: They suggest combining the dependent exemption, child credit, and EITC into a single credit that would initially rise along with earnings, and then phase down to a minimum benefit of $1,270 per child for all families.

Schools, Better and Worse

The most important thing government does for children is fund schools. Families who make use of public elementary and secondary schools receive benefits unavailable to those who choose private schools (except in some states where voucher programs are under way). The average level of government spending per child is currently about $6,000 per year. But levels of spending vary considerably, both across and within states, from more than $8,000 per student to less than $4,000. Because most schools are financed primarily by property taxes, rich communities have rich schools. In comfy suburbs with rising real estate values, even relatively low tax rates can generate high revenues.

Under pressure from grassroots groups, more than a dozen states have moved toward financial equalization in recent years, redistributing funds from rich districts to poor ones. As well, some federal funds (under the Title I program) are targeted specifically to children from low-income families for tutoring and similar programs to improve educational performance. But these redistributional efforts are modest, and it is unlikely that they fully counteract the inequalities built into the larger school finance system. The extent to which such inequalities affect educational outcomes is hotly debated, but many progressive policy makers argue that "leveling up" should be a high priority.

Early education programs offer especially important benefits to children from poor families by improving their reading readiness and better preparing them for the first grade. The Rand Corporation estimates that such programs, targeted to low-income states, would more than pay for their costs. Even the conservative economist James Heckman (recent winner of the Nobel Prize) argues that we should spend more in this area. Yet public investments remain low. Al Gore campaigned on a promise of $50 billion over ten years in matching grants to states, or less than $5 billion a year. George W. Bush mumbled about the possibility of expanding Head Start.

About $4 billion was spent on Head Start in 1998. Despite its political popularity, the program has never enrolled more than about 40 percent of eligible children; and, because it is typically organized on a half-day basis, it does not meet the needs of many mothers who work for pay. Furthermore, as families earn more income, they lose their eligibility for Head Start in a phaseout similar to that of the EITC.

Federal block grants have enabled states to increase spending on child care, but slots remain scarce: Less than 15 percent of families eligible for child-care assistance actually receive it. Efforts have been targeted to mothers leaving the welfare rolls, so almost-but-not-quite-poor families are least likely to receive assistance with child-care costs. Many states have opted for quantity over quality—providing vouchers to large numbers of families but setting voucher levels so low that they cannot pay for high-quality center-based care.

The higher its income, the more likely a family can afford child care with an explicitly educational component. Only about half of four-year-olds from households with incomes of $10,000 or less attend center-based programs. Attendance is even lower among working-poor families who do not qualify for Head Start or state assistance. By contrast, more than 75 percent of four-year-olds from households with incomes of $50,000 or more are learning their ABCs in center-based programs. And affluent parents are more likely to be able to make use of the Child and Dependent Care Credit (which is worth as much as $720 for families with incomes of $75,000 or more with two children). Upscale professional and managerial parents also are well positioned to ask their employers for pretax accounts that allow them to set aside up to $5,000 per year for dependent care; this money is exempt from income and payroll taxes (a subsidy worth about $2,000 a year per child to families in the highest income bracket).

The low level of public support for child care means that in many cities it actually costs more to send a four-year-old to an early education program than to send an eighteen-year-old to college. The subsidies built into community college and state university tuition rates, combined with the extensive financial aid available for enrollment at private colleges, cover about 60 percent of total expenditures. Students at public universities enjoy a subsidy of about 80 percent. In contrast, only about 30 percent of the total costs of child care are subsidized by the government.

This huge difference in public support has momentous distributional implications: Children from low-income families, less likely to graduate from high school and go on to college, are less able to take advantage of higher-education subsidies. In 1992 only about 28 percent of high school graduates from the poorest quartile of families enrolled in a four-year college within twenty months of graduation, compared with 66 percent from the richest quartile. Family income had a significant effect even among graduates with identical high school records and test scores.

Through the Safety Nets

Federal policy provides two different safety nets designed to protect children against economic misfortune. One is survivors' insurance, a feature of Social Security that provides benefits to covered families who suffer the death of a wage earner, with virtually no restrictions. The other is Temporary Assistance for Needy Families (TANF), a welfare program that imposes strict eligibility requirements, time limits, and work requirements. However different these programs may appear, both are funded by tax revenues and both represent a form of social insurance.

The amounts of survivor assistance are generous. In 1997 the average annual benefit per child was $6,012. The average annual benefit per widowed father or mother was $6,264. For a widowed father or mother with two children, the total came to $18,288. Compare this number with the maximum annual TANF benefit in the typical state for a family of three at that time: $4,548. That's less than a third as much. The family receiving survivors' insurance does not have to qualify as poor to receive this help. There is no requirement that the surviving spouse find a job.

Economist Gary Becker, who writes a regular column for *Business Week,* denounces the effect of welfare as follows: "It's bad for children to grow up in a family where all they know is that a check comes from the government every month. That's destructive of the child's self-respect and self-esteem." But is it bad for children or their families to receive survivors' insurance or life insurance money? Or, for that matter, a trust fund check? Do popular magazines or TV shows ever interview young middle-class widows or rich coupon clippers who are ashamed of receiving a monthly check? The amount of federal money docketed for TANF in 1997 was $16.5 billion; state expenditures were about the same, for a total of $33 billion. The amount spent on survivors' insurance that year was about $55 billion.

The bottom line is that we provide more adequate—and more expensive—insurance against the death of a parent than against the desertion or economic inadequacy of a parent, which are the primary reasons single mothers and their children require public assistance. Child-support enforcement efforts have improved but vary enormously from state to state. Private detectives are willing to track down a delinquent parent in return for a percentage of the child support owed—if it's a large amount. Such bounty hunters seldom see low-income parents as attractive clients.

Consider, as well, the way housing policies help different families. A variety of government programs subsidize housing for poor families, and the children in these families benefit. At the same time, families who own their homes can deduct the interest they pay from their taxable income, a benefit that costs the federal government more than twice as much as is spent on low-income housing assistance and low-rent public housing.

Similarly, employer-provided health insurance is tax-exempt—an important benefit for the families of those workers who enjoy it, few of whom are at the bottom of the income distribution. Medicaid has traditionally financed care for poor children. Since 1996 it has been disconnected from welfare, and its coverage has been reduced. An Urban

Institute study shows that many eligible children are not participating, perhaps because their families are unaware of their eligibility. Similarly, the Children's Health Insurance Program (CHIP), enacted in 1997 to help kids whose parents did not qualify for Medicaid and were too poor to afford commercial plans, failed to deliver the goods. A spate of publicity earlier this fall revealed that many states had not fully used the federal funds they were offered. Need was not lacking; political commitment was.

Poverty and Progressivity

Poverty rates in the United States are higher than in any other industrialized country. The reason is simple: We don't provide the level of public assistance that countries such as France and Sweden do. Child poverty rates vary widely within the United States. In the 1990s, they ranged from a low of 6.9 percent in Maryland to a high of 45 percent in Washington, D.C. States with high levels of income inequality among children also have high levels of poverty among children, according to the Urban Institute. Much of this variation is attributable to differences in state "policy effort." In other words, those states that have made concerted efforts to reduce poverty and inequality for kids have succeeded.

But the complexity of our public policies, which include tax benefits and public assistance as well as programs that are actually labeled "insurance," makes it difficult for ordinary citizens to understand who is getting what. Furthermore, the U-shaped pattern of the most visible tax benefits—higher at both ends than in the middle—may undermine support for more generous profamily policies. One way to address this political problem is to fill in the middle—for example, by supporting the proposal for a Universal Unified Child Credit. But it is important to remember that this proposal will do little to directly help children in poor families.

The only true way to build an "opportunity society" is to thoroughly reform our current social insurance and education policies. If we want to link the profamily agenda to the ideal of equal opportunity for kids, we need to explain why some Horatio Algers won't have a chance without some early help from Robin Hood.

Child's Play

Why Universal, High-Quality Day Care Should Be Elementary

JONATHAN COHN

Tracey Hunt, a twenty-eight-year-old single mother living in Boston's Fenway neighborhood, did not want to go back on welfare. She had been there before, about five years ago, while she was pregnant with her second child. Back then, the problem was not a lack of work; it was that the work (waiting tables at a local restaurant) didn't pay enough to justify the cost of day care. And while the restaurant owner thought highly enough of her to offer a promotion to manager, Hunt couldn't accept the post—and the higher salary—because it would have meant finding child care at night, which is prohibitively expensive if you can find it at all. So Hunt reluctantly went onto public assistance, where she benefited from state-subsidized day care and took job-training courses. After ten months, she returned to work, a true welfare-to-work success story.

Only now, five years later, she was back in a familiar bind. For two years she'd been working at a local economic development agency. But now she had another child on the way. And while her salary (approximately $20,000) made her eligible for child-care assistance from the state, there was a waiting list for people like her not currently on welfare. So Hunt had to improvise with unlicensed child-care providers who would take what Hunt could pay. It complicated her job: If the provider was sick or decided to take a vacation, she was stuck. But that wasn't her biggest concern. She had wanted her son in an enriching environment that might develop his cognitive and social abilities for when he started school. She wasn't getting that through informal child care; with one provider, she constantly found her son plopped in front of the television.

The good news is that in late April, after sixteen months of making do, Hunt's son finally did make it off the waiting list for a well-regarded child-care center in nearby Mission Hill. The bad news is that about 19,000 more children were still on the list—with waits as long as two years. For the most part, the parents of these children don't want to be on public assistance: Like Tracey Hunt, they are eager and willing to work. But many end up on (or back on) welfare because child-care costs overwhelm their meager paychecks. Many lose jobs because they skipped too many days taking care of sick kids. Many can't take night classes to get better jobs because nighttime child care is so expensive or unavailable. And many leave their children in less-than-ideal day-care arrangements that, at best, are merely safe and clean—thus diminishing the chances that their children will eventually make their way up the income ladder.

An Empty Consensus

When Congress took up welfare reform in 1996, there was heated debate over many issues. But a surprising number of Democrats and Republicans agreed, at least in principle, on more investment in child care: If parents couldn't find affordable, high-quality care for their kids once they entered the workforce, they wouldn't be able to hold on to their jobs—let alone move on to better ones. And if the next generation didn't get high-quality care while their mothers adapted to paid work, the cycle would be more likely to repeat itself. So leaders in both parties promised that, as part of the welfare overhaul, they would increase spending on child care.

Four years into the welfare reform experiment, the federal government has indeed increased child-care outlays. The 1996 welfare reform law consolidated four separate programs into one Child Care and Development Block Grant. While an easing of regulations has allowed states to get away with spending less of their own money, the net result is still more total spending on child care. After two years of welfare reform, a General Accounting Office survey of seven states showed total government outlay on child care up by an average of 24 percent. Since then, as the welfare rolls have declined, even more money has become available, since states may transfer money earmarked for welfare checks into subsidies for child care.

But this extra money is not enough. Only about one person in ten technically eligible for some kind of public assistance for child care actually receives it, according to the best available estimate from the federal government. While that clearly doesn't mean that 90 percent of kids in low-income families get no care at all—many find care through informal family arrangements, as Tracey Hunt did—the long waiting lists for subsidized care in states like California (200,000) and Texas (37,000) suggest that many families who really could use the help don't get it.

And those numbers refer only to the people who meet the guidelines for state subsidies. Millions more make too much to qualify but find the cost of care—not to mention the difficulty of finding it—has them pinned in the lower-middle class. Indeed, while 10 million children now qualify for assistance under existing state guidelines, the U.S. Department of Health and Human Services estimates the number would grow to around 15 million if all states set their eligibility limits at the maximum level allowed under federal law, which is itself modest.

Custodial Care, Enriching Care

Access to affordable care is only half the problem. Children from lower-income families are far less likely to come from stable homes surrounded by nurturing communities than their middle-class counterparts. An ideal assistance program would provide them not just with child care but with quality care—the kind that gives them sustained, personal attention; the kind that teaches them the basic skills that will allow them to keep pace in elementary school and, eventually, to compete in a skills-driven economy. Yet, based on any number of indicators, low-income children are far less likely to get that kind of care: Except for the lucky ones who make it into Head Start—the federally funded, full-service preschool program tailored for the children of families below the poverty line (Head Start serves just half of eligible families)—many of the rest end up in poorly supervised, unstimulating environments.

This failure casts welfare reform in a less flattering light. The standard yardstick for progress—the declining welfare rolls and the number of former welfare recipients who find work—doesn't capture the lingering impact on children left in substandard care or the extent to which former welfare recipients get stuck in bad jobs in order to accommodate day-care schedules.

But it would be a mistake to blame the child-care crisis on welfare reform itself. After all, the lack of affordable, high-quality day care was a problem long before Bill Clinton and the Republican Congress killed the old welfare system. Welfare reform perhaps made the child-care problem more acute by pushing women into the workforce faster, thus adding to the strain on an already burdened system. But it's not responsible for creating this problem in the first place. And, anyway, getting more parents to work was ostensibly the goal of welfare policy even before the 1996 overhaul.

Indeed, policy makers interested in addressing this problem should pan back and view it not merely as a problem with the welfare system but as a problem that affects the entire lower-income and working-class population. That's the paradox of the child-care crisis: The fact that it is much, much more extensive than typically understood also means the coalition-building necessary to solve the problem might be just a little bit easier than many people think, given some imagination and political leadership.

Massachusetts provides a good case study. Total in-state spending on child care has increased dramatically since welfare reform passed six years ago, up to $500 million a year from $200 million in 1996. Much of that increase reflects new federal spending. Overall, Massachusetts, like most states, now spends less of its own money on welfare than it did before welfare reform passed. Still, under pressure from child-advocacy groups, Massachusetts has increased its contribution to child care in the past two years.

The state delivers most of this money to recipients in two different ways. Some of it goes to vouchers, which parents can use to pay for child care by any accredited provider, whether it's a large day-care center that serves forty or a home-based care provider who takes care of four. Nearly all the rest is spent on direct contracts with child-care providers, who then agree to provide care to low-income residents either free or at reduced rates (according to a sliding scale based on income). The fact that Massachusetts still has this mix is but one way the state's system is superior to many others. Other states have moved entirely to a system of vouchers, largely because it is easier to give people vouchers than to go out and make agreements with child-care providers. Yet part of the problem with child care is that, in many low-income communities, there just aren't enough providers—or, at least, there aren't enough providers willing to accept vouchers (which often do not pay as well as parents paying on their own). By signing some contracts with providers, Massachusetts can help improve the supply of child care as well as subsidizing the parents who must pay for it.

And yet, for all of this well-designed investment, Massachusetts still falls far short of serving everybody who is eligible for help, much less the broader pool of the working poor. Under state law, anybody who makes less than 50 percent of the state median income—or about $32,000 a year for a family of four—can receive vouchers or enroll their children in contract slots. (Until May 2000, the figure was around $27,500; Massachusetts hadn't adjusted the levels since 1992.) But qualifying for one of these subsidies or slots doesn't guarantee you'll get one. Simply put, the state doesn't spend enough money to serve the entire eligible population.

So Massachusetts gives priority to people who are on welfare but trying to get off. The state guarantees a child care voucher for only one year after a family goes off welfare. After that, it's first come, first served, until the money runs out. "A good thing about child-care policy is that the state has tried to address the needs of families leaving welfare," says Elaine Fersh, director of Boston-based Parents United for Child Care. "But it has really pitted those folks against those who were low income—fought hard not to go on welfare, but didn't get subsidies." All told, reports the U.S. Department of Health and Human Services, just 15 percent of the state's eligible population is receiving some sort of assistance for child care. And, again, that doesn't include the tens of thousands more who make too much to qualify but, given the ludicrously high cost of child care, need the help anyway.

Parents do find ways to cope, of course. But the arrangements are often lacking. Two years ago, Parents United for Child Care commissioned a scientific survey of parents by researchers from the University of Massachusetts, Boston. The results, published April 2000 in a report called "Choices and Tradeoffs," confirmed that children from low-income families are, on the whole, much less likely to end up in quality care settings. For example, just 32 percent of preschool-age children from low-income families were in licensed, center-based day care (which tends to be of higher quality, more geared toward developing cognitive and social skills)—compared to 42 percent from middle-income families and 54 percent from high-income families. (Many upper-income families had stay-at-home moms, nannies, or both.)

Not surprisingly, the survey also found that low-income parents were having to make much greater career sacrifices in order to manage day care. One-third reported having to quit a job because they couldn't find child care to meet the job schedule or because the job wasn't flexible enough; 13 percent said they actually lost jobs because of child-care problems. More than one-fourth said that, at one point, they went on welfare specifically because it was the only way to get affordable child care. Of the parents surveyed who were currently unemployed, 30 percent said they would "very likely" get work or go to school—if only they had access to quality child care they could afford.

Needed: A Comprehensive System

Behind this dilemma lies a largely unappreciated chicken-and-egg problem. There's an enormous social demand for quality day care. But the low purchasing power of poor families and the paucity of government subsidies understate the effective economic demand. So even if the state did make the money for vouchers and contracts available, it wouldn't solve the problem, especially at current reimbursement rates, because there aren't enough child-care providers to take care of the state's population. Nationally, the average salary for child-care workers is around $14,500—less than what janitors or bartenders make—and at that salary, it's hard to recruit new workers, to say nothing of keeping current ones. (About one-third of child-care workers leave their jobs after a year, according to the Labor Department.)

Consider the infant and toddler population, traditionally the hardest and most expensive to serve: In 1999, there were about 235,000 such children in Massachusetts, but just 35,000 licensed day-care slots—and just 10,000 public subsidies. "There are people who have offered me bribes," says Patty Bradley, whose East Boston Social Center serves about 250 and has a wait list of 500. "There just isn't enough child care to go around."

In all these respects, Massachusetts mirrors what is happening in the nation at large. In most states, there is more child-care money available now than there was before welfare reform. And in the best day-care states, such as Wisconsin, the state government has aggressively sought to provide a seamless web of child-care services both for those on welfare and for those coming off. But Wisconsin is the exception. Florida, for example, has not only seen its federal child-care money increase; it has spent more money of its own, too. Yet it still has 13,000 children on its wait list.

Things are even worse in the states less committed to spending their own money. Connecticut hasn't adjusted its payments to child-care providers in nearly ten years, which is one reason just 13 percent of eligible parents receive assistance. In Minneapolis, according to one study, one-fourth of the single mothers who went back on welfare after leaving the rolls did so because they couldn't afford child care—and couldn't get off the waiting lists. A new study by Bruce Fuller from the University of California, Berkeley, and Sharon Lynn Kagan of Yale looked at 1,000 single mothers leaving the welfare rolls in California, Connecticut, and Florida. They found that the majority of the children were in low-quality settings and were already lagging behind national norms on cognitive skills (though, in fairness, they couldn't yet determine to what extent the substandard child care was responsible for the lag).

What would a comprehensive solution to this problem look like? For starters, it would have to attack the problem from two directions: boosting the ability of low-income families to afford child care while also increasing the supply of high-quality child-care providers to meet the demand. The former would involve vastly expanding the investment in child-care subsidies; the latter, spending more money not just on reimbursement rates to child-care providers but also on the construction of facilities that could house day-care centers, particularly in low-income communities. The common ingredient in all of this is—what else?—money. Isabel Sawhill of the Brookings Institution has estimated that it would cost about $30 billion a year to finance a high-quality, two-year preschool program. Other estimates have pegged the number closer to $40 billion.

Compared to the costs of forcing low-income parents to choose between success at work and conscientious child rearing, this is not too high a price to bear. Remember, most states today spend less of their own money on welfare than they did before welfare reform. Since quality child care puts children from low-income families on a course for more economically productive lives, money spent on it now is money not spent on public assistance—or throwing delinquents in jail—later. You can take this argument one step further and argue that with better-paying jobs, these kids will eventually generate more tax revenue. Even if this doesn't make child care a break-even proposition, as some of the more enthusiastic advocates claim, it would temper the cost significantly.

A New Politics of Child Care

As a political matter, certainly, thinking bigger can have its advantages. Just consider what Georgia did with preschool. In 1995, rather than simply increase the spending targeted at the state's low-income population, Democratic governor Zell Miller proposed making preschool universal—that is, available to anybody who wanted it, for free. This meant spending a great deal more money on the program—more than

$200 million a year. But it also meant getting many more people behind the idea. The program has been a dramatic success.

Today, more than 60,000 children attend publicly financed preschool in Georgia, with polls showing four of five voters in favor of continuing the program. There's no reason similar logic can't apply at a national level. Yes, the money will have to come from somewhere. But given the experience in Georgia (not the most left-wing of states), it's not entirely unthinkable that a persuasive candidate could make a compelling case to finance a universal preschool program. (In case you are wondering, Miller chose to finance it through the lottery—and, unlike officials in other states who ostensibly dedicated lottery funds to education, Miller didn't then cut back on education spending from other sources.)

There is also a precedent, albeit an old one, for doing this sort of thing on the national level: the turn-of-the-century kindergarten movement. As with day care, the creation of free, tax-supported kindergarten was controversial in part because some people thought it was inherently bad for children—and in part because it was seen, initially, as a program designed primarily to help the children of low-income immigrant families. (The fact that the idea of kindergarten—the word itself was foreign—was imported from Europe didn't help this impression.) But as Barbara Beatty shows in *Preschool Education in America*, when middle-class families began to see kindergarten as a potentially enriching experience for their children, too, they lent their crucial political support, which was instrumental in making kindergarten widely available to all comers. Since the vast majority of mothers from all socioeconomic classes now work and need day care, there's no reason a national preschool movement couldn't coalesce in the very same way.

During the 2000 election campaign Vice President Al Gore waded into these waters. He proposed making preschool universal nationally. Of course, he had not fleshed out his plan with details, and the small federal contribution to this effort he proposed would have been too meager. Nevertheless, it at least suggested he understood the problem. That's more than can be said for George W. Bush. As a candidate, Bush spent a great deal of time complaining about "toll booths" on the road to prosperity—obstacles that keep poor and working-class Americans from making it into the middle class. Yet he had almost nothing to say about spending more money on child care—which, as Tracey Hunt and at least 19,000 other Massachusetts parents can tell you, is often the real obstacle on the road to prosperity.

Support for Working Families

What We Can Learn from Europe about Family Policies

JANET C. GORNICK AND

MARCIA K. MEYERS

F our decades of steady growth in female employment have gone a long way toward closing the job gap between women and men in the industrialized countries. One of the most striking changes in Europe and the United States has been the rise in employment among mothers with young children. Nearly 85 percent of U.S. mothers employed before childbearing now return to work before their child's first birthday. Although this is an encouraging trend from the perspective of gender equality in the marketplace, it is raising a new and difficult question about arrangements in the home: If everyone is working in the market, who is caring for the children?

Many parents in the industrialized countries find themselves navigating uncertain new terrain between a society that expects women to bear the primary responsibility for caring in the home and a society that expects, and increasingly requires, all adults to be at work in the market.

Mothers and fathers are struggling to craft private solutions to this problem. But rather than resolving the question of who will care for children when everyone is on the job, these private solutions often exacerbate gender inequality, overburden the parents, and ultimately lead to poor-quality child care.

Although such problems are not unique to the United States, they may be more acute in this country because families have access to so little public support. The nation's policy makers and opinion leaders have been preoccupied in recent years with the promotion of "family values." Compared with most of Europe, however, this country provides exceptionally meager help to children, their parents, and the workers—mostly women—who care for other people's children. And despite the current preoccupation with getting everyone—particularly poor mothers—into the workforce, the United States does much less than European countries to remove employment barriers for women with young children.

The Problem of Private Solutions

One private solution to child care adopted by many parents in the United States is the combining of parental caregiving and part-time employment. Because the parents who work reduced hours are overwhelmingly mothers—only 42 percent of American women work full time year-round—this solution exacerbates gender inequality in both the market and the caring spheres. Part-time work schedules, career interruptions, and intermittent employment relegate many women to the least remunerative and rewarding jobs; and these employment patterns contribute to wage penalties that persist long after the children are grown. In dual-parent families with children below school age, married mothers' labor-market income accounts for, at most, a third of families' total labor-market income across the industrialized countries; in the United States, it accounts for only one-quarter.

Another private solution is the combining of substitute care for children and full-time parental employment. Although this works well for some families, many others find themselves overburdened by the demands of the market and the home. Women in particular often work the equivalent of a double shift, combining full-time paid work with unpaid caregiving. In a recent article in *Demography,* Suzanne Bianchi concludes that despite the increase in mothers' labor-market activities, their time spent with their children remained nearly constant between 1965 and 1998. Where do employed mothers get the time? The data suggest that they do less of everything else, including housework, volunteering, engaging in leisure activities, and sleeping.

More parental employment also means children spend much more time in substitute care. Recent increases in the use of child care in the United States have been particularly sharp for children below age one, 44 percent of whom are now in some form of nonparental child care. The extensive reliance on substitute child care imposes a heavy financial burden, consuming as much as 35 percent of household income for poor working families. It also raises concerns about the quality of care in children's youngest and most developmentally sensitive years. These concerns are particularly acute in the United States, where experts conclude that nearly two-thirds of the mostly private nonparental child-care settings provide only fair to poor care.

The private child-care solution to the work-family dilemma creates another, often overlooked problem: It impoverishes a large, low-wage child-care workforce dominated by women. Child-care workers in the

United States are among the most poorly paid members of the workforce, averaging less than $7 per hour in earnings and usually working without employment benefits or realistic opportunities for career advancement.

While parents in the United States are left largely to their own devices, parents in most European welfare states can count on child-care and parental-leave benefits to help them juggle work in the market and in the home. Although these policies have not fully resolved the problems of gender inequality and parental overburdening, they provide encouraging lessons about how government can help parents strike a balance between caring and earning.

Key to realizing greater gender equality in both the workplace and the home is recognizing that mothers and fathers alike deserve support in their market and caregiving roles. For a number of years, feminist scholars in Europe and the United States have debated the meaning of a woman-friendly welfare state. A universal-breadwinner perspective calls for welfare-state provisions that support and equalize women's employment attachments—for example, by providing extensive public child care. An opposing caregiver-parity perspective calls for provisions that grant women "the right to time for care" and remunerate women for care work performed in the home through generous maternity pay and other caregiver benefits.

Neither perspective fully resolves the tension between work and family life while promoting gender equality. Both fail to provide a satisfying vision of the welfare state—in part because they do not address the issue of fathers as caregivers. Women's widespread assumption of greater market responsibilities has not been equally matched by fathers' assumption of child-care responsibilities in the home. Although men's involvement in caregiving appears to be on the rise, Bianchi estimates that married fathers in the United States spent just 45 percent of the time their wives spent on caregiving in 1998—an increase of only 15 percentage points since 1965.

A bridge between the universal-breadwinner and caregiver-parity perspectives may lie in social policies that promote what British welfare-state scholar Rosemary Crompton calls the "dual earner/dual carer" society. This is a society in which men and women engage symmetrically in both paid work in the labor market and caregiving work in the home. Central to the dual earner/dual carer solution is the recognition that *both* mothers and fathers should have the right and opportunity to engage in market and caregiving work without incurring poverty in terms of money or time. For families with very young children (say, younger than age three), mothers and fathers would have the right to take substantial time off from market work to care for their children, without loss of income. For families with children from age three to school age, both parents would have the right to engage in flexible and reduced-hour employment, and they would have access to affordable, high-quality substitute child care.

This solution assumes that men would reallocate substantial portions of time from the labor market to the home while their children are young. Hence, as American political theorist Nancy Fraser has suggested, "men [would] become more like women are now" in the allocation of their time.

The sweeping transformations of market and gender relations necessary to achieve a gender-egalitarian dual earner/dual carer society are obviously not imminent. But the steep rise in maternal employment in recent years and the more modest rise in men's caregiving time suggest that some form of dual earner/dual carer arrangement is already the reality for many families in the industrialized world. Given this reality, what can government do to help such families now and to promote greater gender equality in the future? The United States is arguably a leader in rhetorical support for the family and for equal employment opportunities, but it's a clear laggard in making the rhetoric meaningful. U.S. policy makers could take a lesson from the European welfare states, which finance extensive parental leaves during the earliest years of children's lives and provide high-quality early-childhood education and care services for older preschool children. Increasingly, these countries also incorporate incentives that encourage men to assume a larger share of caregiving work in the home.

Family Leave

Although their family-support programs vary substantially, nearly all of the industrialized welfare states provide generous maternity, paternity, or other parental leave during the first year of childhood, typically funded through some combination of national sickness, maternity, and other social-insurance funds. The most substantial leave benefits are provided in two Scandinavian countries that have consolidated maternity, paternity, and other parental-leave schemes. Norwegian parents are entitled to share fifty-two weeks of leave with an 80-percent wage replacement (or forty-two weeks with full wage replacement) following the birth of a child, while Swedish parents can share a full year of leave with nearly full wage replacement, followed by three additional months at a lower rate. Most Continental European countries provide somewhat shorter maternity leaves—usually three to five months—but they pay relatively high replacement rates: 80 percent to 100 percent.

Even beyond the child's first birthday, parents in some European countries have rights to partial leave and reduced-hour employment. In Denmark, for example, mothers have a right to twenty-eight weeks of maternity leave after childbirth with high wage replacement, and fathers have a right to two weeks of paternity leave; once these leaves are exhausted, the parents can share ten weeks of parental leave with high wage replacement, and then each parent is entitled to thirteen weeks of child-care leave at 80 percent of the parental-leave benefit level. Finnish parents can choose to stay on leave for up to three years while receiving a low, flat-rate benefit. And Swedish parents have the right to work as little as six hours per week, with job protection, until their children are eight years old.

Although generous leave policies have economic and social benefits for families with very young children, they can create new forms of gender inequality. The total percentage of paid parental-leave days taken by fathers amounts to less than 10 percent across the European welfare states and less than 3 percent in many. Because leaves are taken overwhelmingly by mothers, many women pay a price for their long absences from the labor market in the form of lost human capital and career advancement.

Several of the Scandinavian countries are addressing the gender gap in parental-leave taking by creating incentives for fathers to take the leave to which they are entitled. The most critical of these incentives is high wage-replacement rates. Because men tend to have higher wages than women, in the absence of full wage replacement, it often makes economic sense for couples to decide that the mother should withdraw from the labor market. The 80 percent to 100 percent wage-replacement rates in most of the European countries reduce the economic disincentive for fathers to take full advantage of leave benefits.

A second important gender-equalizing policy is the granting of individual or nontransferable leave benefits to fathers as well as to mothers. In Norway and Sweden, four weeks of parental leave are reserved explicitly for fathers; in Denmark fathers have a right to two weeks of paternity leave. In all three countries, leave time reserved for the father but not taken is lost to the family. These "use or lose" provisions encourage parents to participate more equally in leave-supported caregiving. The Scandinavian welfare states have taken active steps to promote fathers' use of leave benefits. In the late 1990s, the Swedish government engaged in a public campaign to educate employers and unions about how fathers' parental leave can be good not just for families but for work organizations and society. Norwegian policy expert Anne Lise Ellingsaeter reports that in her country government officials are now pushing fatherhood onto the political agenda: "While employment for women was the main issue of policies in the 1980s," she suggests, the 1990s brought in "the caring father, and thus the domestication of men." The emphasis on fathers is expanding beyond the Scandinavian countries as well. Italy, for example, instituted use-or-lose days in 2000.

The European welfare states also provide instructive lessons about how to finance parental-leave benefits. Nearly all of the European leave programs are funded through either social-insurance schemes or general tax revenues. None relies on mandating employers to provide wage replacement for their own employees. Those countries in which social-insurance funds draw heavily on employer contributions do not "experience-rate"—that is, adjust contributions to reflect the number of leave takers at the firm level. These financing mechanisms reduce employer resistance by spreading the cost among employers and by supplementing employer contributions with general revenue funds. By

reducing the cost to individual employers, these mechanisms also minimize the risk that employers will discriminate against potential leave
takers who might otherwise be seen as unusually expensive employees.

How costly are these leave schemes? Spending on maternity, paternity, and parental leave is substantial and is rising in nearly all the European welfare states. Costs relative to population and gross domestic
product (GDP) are surprisingly modest, however. As of the middle
1990s, annual family leave expenditures per employed woman (in 1990
U.S. dollars) were about $900 in Sweden and Finland, and about $600 to
$700 in Norway and Denmark. France spent a more moderate $375 per
employed woman. The higher-spending Scandinavian countries invested approximately 0.7 percent to 1.0 percent of GDP in family leave,
while France spent 0.35 percent.

Child Care

The European welfare states provide another critical form of support
for dual earner/dual carer families and for gender equality in the form
of high-quality, public early-childhood education and care. They have
developed two distinct models. The model in the Scandinavian countries is an integrated system of child-care centers and organized family
day-care schemes serving children from birth to school age, managed
by social-welfare or educational authorities. Nearly all employed parents have access to a place in the public child-care system with little or
no waiting time, and enrollment rates are high. In Sweden and Denmark, for example, one-third to one-half of children under age three are
in some form of full-day, publicly supported care, along with 72 percent
to 82 percent of children between the ages of three and five.

The model developed by the Continental countries of France and Belgium is a two-phase system of child care. For younger children, full-day child-care centers (*creches*) and some publicly supervised family day-care schemes are provided under the authority of the social-welfare system. Beginning at age two and a half or three, children are served in full-day preprimary programs, the *écoles maternelles,* within the educational system. Enrollment of young children in *creches* is high (30 percent in Belgium and 24 percent in France); it's nearly universal in the *écoles maternelles* for preschool-age children.

Although a large child-care sector would seem to be unambiguously positive for gender equality in employment, it can exacerbate inequality if it impoverishes women who work as child-care providers. In the European countries, although the child-care sector is also predominantly female, a large share of child-care workers are public-sector employees. As such, they benefit from the good public-sector wages and benefits common in Europe. Relatively high wages for child-care workers are tied to high standards for the education and training of childcare professionals, who are typically required to have three to five years of vocational or university training. Higher educational standards have benefits that extend beyond the economic welfare of female child-care workers. They also increase the quality of care that children receive.

Like leave benefits, early-childhood education and care services in European countries are financed largely by the government. Funding is provided by national, state or regional, and local authorities, with the national share typically dominant in services for preschool-age children. Care for very young children and, to a lesser extent, for preschool children is partially funded through parental co-payments that cover an average of 15 percent to 25 percent of costs. Because co-payments are scaled to family income, lower-income families typically pay nothing and more affluent families pay no more than 10 percent to 15 percent of their income.

Child-care expenditures are large and growing in the European welfare states but, like leave expenditures, are modest in per capita terms. Total spending on direct child care in the mid-1990s was about $2,000 per child under age fifteen in Sweden and Denmark; it served a large share of all children under the age of seven and many school-aged children in after-school care. In France expenditures totaled a little over $1,000 per child under age fifteen; they served nearly all three-to-five-year-olds and about one-quarter of children under age three. These investments in early-childhood education and care constituted about 1.6 percent to 2.2 percent of GDP in Sweden and Denmark, and about 1 percent in France.

On all fronts, the United States lags behind Europe to a remarkable extent. The United States stands out as one of only a few countries in the entire world that fail to provide any national program of paid maternity leave. Until 1993 this country lacked even job protections for women at the time of childbirth. With the passage of the Family and Medical Leave Act (FMLA), workers in firms with at least fifty employees were granted rights to twelve weeks of unpaid, job-protected leave each year for childbirth, adoption, or to care for a seriously ill family member. The exclusion of small firms leaves an estimated one-half of the U.S. workforce without even this rudimentary benefit. Additionally, the absence of wage replacement presents an obvious problem: The congressionally established U.S. Commission on Leave reports that 64 percent of employees who need but do not take FMLA-based leave indicate that they cannot afford the loss of wages.

Some families in the United States receive short periods of paid leave through employer-based disability benefits. Five states provide public Temporary Disability Insurance (TDI) programs. Because the Pregnancy Discrimination Act applies to these programs, new mothers have a right to short periods of paid leave if they have either private or public disability benefits. As of the early 1990s, however, only an estimated one-quarter of working women in the United States had coverage under these laws. The Institute for Women's Policy Research found that weekly benefits paid through the TDI programs average only $170 to $200 and that the duration of benefit claims ranged from five to thirteen weeks.

The United States also stands out among industrialized countries for its paucity of public child-care assistance. Unlike most of Europe, it has never embraced a national system for universal provision, funding, or regulation of early-childhood education and care. More than 40 percent of American children under age five spend thirty-five hours or more per week in nonparental care, and another 25 percent spend fifteen to thirty-five hours.

Substitute care in this country is overwhelmingly private in both provision and financing. The U.S. government spends about $200 on direct child-care assistance per child under age fifteen—about one-tenth of the spending in Sweden and one-fifth of that in France. Assistance is provided through two primary mechanisms: (1) means-tested subsidies, available on a limited basis for low-income families with employed parents; and (2) early-childhood education programs (mostly through the means-tested Head Start program) and state prekindergarten programs. Children in the United States now routinely start public school at a young age; about one-half of four-year-olds and 89 percent of five-year-olds are in (usually) part-day prekindergarten or kindergarten programs. But as few as 5 percent of children age three and younger, and of older preschool children outside prekindergarten and kindergarten, are in any form of publicly subsidized or provided care.

Some observers justify miserly child-care expenditures in the United States by pointing to tax benefits for families who use child care. The federal government and several state governments exempt a portion of child-care expenses from personal income taxes. While the federal Child and Dependent Care Credit is now used by a large number of families, low-income families with no tax liability receive no benefits, and the actual benefit for others is low. As of the mid-1990s, the federal tax credit expenditures totaled about $47 per child under the age of fifteen.

Unfortunately, the United States gets what it pays for. Minimally regulated private child-care arrangements provide uneven and generally low-quality care. A research team from the National Institute of Child Health and Human Development recently estimated that only 11 percent of child-care settings for children age three and younger meet standards for "excellent" care. In part, quality is poor because the care is provided by a minimally educated and inadequately trained workforce. According to data collected by Marcy Whitebook of the Center for the Child Care Workforce, some 22 percent to 34 percent of teachers in regulated child-care centers and family child-care settings do not have a high school diploma; Ellen Galinsky, president of the Families and Work Institute, reports that in unregulated family-and-relative child-care settings, between 33 percent and 46 percent of caregivers have not completed high school.

Child-care providers are a poorly educated workforce in large part because families cannot afford to pay more highly trained professionals. Full-time child care for a four-year-old averages between $3,500 and

$6,000 per year—more than college tuition at many state universities. Yet, despite this expense, child-care workers often earn poverty-level wages. Whitebook estimates that they earn an average of $6.12 per hour—slightly less than parking-lot attendants and one-third the average salary of flight attendants.

Many of these poorly paid child-care workers are women of color. And many are immigrants from developing countries who are in search of better economic prospects—and who often leave the care of their own children to even poorer women in their home countries.

Although the European welfare states could teach the United States much about child care, they have not completely solved the dilemma of providing gender-egalitarian support for dual earner/dual carer families. The supply of child care for children under age three is very limited in many countries, and for older preschool children in some. Also, both short- and longer-term leaves are still used overwhelmingly by mothers. A fully egalitarian package of family-support policies is not completely realized even in the progressive Scandinavian countries, but there at least the framework for such policies is in place.

Learning across borders may have considerable cachet in contemporary policy debates, but drawing lessons from the European welfare states has fallen out of favor. Resistance to lessons from overseas has been fueled by vivid press reports of the collapse of the European welfare states. American reporters, particularly in the mainstream print and financial media, have been preoccupied in recent years with the death of the European welfare state. In 1992 the *Los Angeles Times* noted that "Britain . . . finished dismantling much of its welfare system in the 1980s under former Prime Minister Margaret Thatcher." The *San Francisco Chronicle* reported in 1993 that "nowhere is the dismantling of the social security net more drastic than in Sweden, [though] similar retreats from the expansive days of social democracy are under way in virtually every European Community nation." And in 1995 *Business Week* reported that "France ... in recent weeks has been at the center of what may well be the last great Continental convulsion in this century: the dismantling of the European welfare state."

The Popular Welfare State

As Mark Twain is said to have observed about premature rumors of his demise, reports of the death of the European welfare state turn out to be greatly exaggerated. Spending trends in Europe suggest that while some countries have taken steps to curtail certain areas of program growth, overall social spending continued to rise throughout the 1980s and 1990s. Growth in expenditure was particularly steep in programs that support families and children. Between 1980 and the mid-1990s, per-child spending on family policy in the Western European countries increased by 52 percent. Within the arena of family policy, the growth in expenditures on maternity and parental leaves was quite high: Across Western Europe, average spending per employed woman doubled during this period.

Rising investments indicate that political support for family policies is strong in the European countries—a finding that is confirmed by public-opinion research. Family policies are popular mostly because they are universally available. Family leave and child care have been institutionalized as middle-class benefits that support new parents, relieve parents of the financial burden of private child care, and provide high-quality early education for children—all without stigmatizing or isolating recipients. The public sees these programs as providing broader social benefits as well. Cross-national policy research has linked generous leave and child-care benefits in Europe to much lower child poverty rates than in the United States, and to less disruption in employment among mothers with young children.

Steadily growing investments in family policies suggest that the European welfare states remain committed to supporting dual earner/dual carer families. Translating these policies to the U.S. context remains challenging. One obvious concern is expense. One way to approach the question of cost is through a thought experiment: What if the United States were to commit the same share of its GDP to family policy as the Europeans do? This country currently spends about 0.2 percent of its GDP on child care and a negligible amount on leave. In contrast, France spends about 1.4 percent of its GDP on a generous policy package of family leave and early-childhood education and care. If the same spending share were applied to the U.S. GDP, we'd be looking at about $100 billion annually. As of the mid-1990s, U.S. expenditures on early-childhood education and care totaled only about $15 billion. Thus, in order to provide a package of leave and child-care benefits similar to the one available to French families, we would need an additional $85 billion per year.

This figure very likely represents a high-end estimate. The actual bill would probably be lower than these figures suggest, since children generally start school at a younger age in the United States than in France. It would also be lower if financing similar benefits consumed a smaller share of the GDP in the strong U.S. economy. Costs would be lower still if policies were partially means-tested or taxed for higher-income families. And recent research suggests that some of those expenditures would be recouped by productivity gains associated with lower employee turnover, fewer work absences, and a less stressed-out workforce.

Nevertheless, it is clear that comprehensive family policies would require substantial new investments in the United States. Whether these investments are affordable is a relative question. It is easy to find examples of spending that might be used to offset new investments in family policy. According to the Center for Popular Economics, federal aid to U.S. corporations amounts to $75 billion to $200 billion a year. Former assistant secretary of defense Lawrence Korb and the Center for Defense Information (founded by retired generals and admirals) have argued that the U.S. military budget could be cut by more than $150 billion a year without sacrificing high levels of military readiness. The United States could also find family policy revenues closer to home, by capping a variety of federal tax benefits that primarily reach our most affluent citizens. The mortgage-interest deduction alone costs nearly $60 billion a year, local property-tax deductions for homeowners cost $14 billion, and the exclusion of capital gains on inherited property costs $25 billion. (See Nancy Folbre's article "Leave No Child Behind?")

Providing real support for America's working families would require an exercise of collective political will. Fortunately, there are some hopeful signs. As more and more families find themselves squeezed for time between the demands of the workplace and the home, support for more expansive family policies may be growing, especially as parents find their budgets squeezed by the price of even mediocre child care. A recent survey conducted for the think tank Zero To Three found that four in five adults support "paid parental leave that allows working parents of very young babies to stay home from work to care for their children." Policy officials are taking at least tentative steps in the direction of policy expansion. Forty-two states now have some form of prekindergarten services. In June 2000, the U.S. Department of Labor issued regulations that allow states to extend unemployment insurance to mothers out of work owing to childbirth. By cross-national standards, these developments are meager. But they may signal a welcome shift in the United States from rhetoric to action in the valuing of children, families, and equal opportunities for women.

Martha Jernegons's New Shoes

The Contribution of Local Living-Wage Ordinances

DAVID MOBERG

Last fall, Martha Jernegons got a raise. By the standards of the new dot-com economy, it wasn't much—just $2.15 per hour. But for Jernegons, a fifty-six-year-old home health-care aide in Chicago, working for a private agency that is reimbursed by the city, it was a 40 percent increase, to $7.60 an hour. Though she still lives below the poverty line—and still lacks health insurance—with a daughter and six grandchildren, that $2.15 an hour made a big difference. She's finally paying off an old $600 medical bill that had been hanging over her for years. "The raise gave me a different outlook on life," she said. "I feel better about myself. Now I can go to Payless and buy a pair of shoes."

Jernegons's shoes are courtesy of Chicago's "living wage" ordinance, which required certain contractors for the city to pay a minimum of $7.60 an hour to its employees. Mayor Richard Daley had resisted the local living-wage coalition of unions, community groups, homeless advocates, and religious organizations, claiming their proposal would break the city budget and drive jobs out of the city. But when he tried to raise salaries for himself and the city council, the coalition effectively seized the moment to demand pay increases for low-wage contract workers as well.

The living-wage movement is one of the nation's strongest grass-roots political reactions to more than a quarter-century of rising economic inequality. Over the past six years, forty-one local governments have passed some form of living-wage legislation. Although the laws vary greatly, most require at least some taxpayer-subsidized employers—mainly service contractors, but also businesses that receive government subsidies and tax breaks or lease public land—to pay substantially more than minimum wages, usually around or somewhat above $8.20 an hour, indexed to keep up with inflation ($8.20 an hour is the amount that enables a full-time worker to earn the poverty level for a family of four). More than half the ordinances also require or encourage health insurance, and a few create a favorable climate for unionization. Since the first living-wage victory, in Baltimore in 1994, the idea has captured the imagination of organizers across the country. There are ongoing campaigns to enforce and expand existing ordinances as well as efforts to enact a living wage in another seventy-five cities.

Despite the energy unleashed across the country by the living-wage idea, the movement has so far directly benefited only a tiny portion of the low-wage workforce—perhaps as few as 46,000 people. (To put this in some perspective, more than 28 million Americans earn less than $8 an hour.) These numbers, however, understate the potential of the movement. For example, San Francisco's proposed ordinance alone would cover 30,000 workers. And as the number of beneficiaries grows, spillover pressure to raise wages could help some workers not directly covered by the laws. Also, even though early proposals typically only pushed pay up to around $7.50 (what the federal minimum wage would be if its value had not been eroded by inflation over the past three decades), the movement is now setting its sights higher, seeking wage floors as high as $12 an hour, or close to what the federal minimum wage would be today if it had also been adjusted for increases in productivity since the late 1960s.

Yet, even beyond the wage hikes, living-wage movements are already influencing political debates, electing local candidates, recasting local economic development strategies, slowing privatization, and fostering unionization. The demand for a living wage is even beginning to spread to state and federal governments and, beyond the public sector, to employees of universities and religious bodies. It is also strengthening bonds among labor, church, and community groups. In fact, the living-wage strategy's greatest achievement may be the creation of a grassroots movement to challenge the still-growing inequality in American society.

The Story So Far

The living wage rejects the notion that the dictates of the market should dominate workers' lives and livelihoods. The demand for a living wage first emerged in the 1870s as an alternative to the labor movement's goal of abolishing "wage slavery" and creating a society of independent producers and cooperatives. The idea was that wage labor could be acceptable if it supported a family and provided a standard of living that reflected American cultural expectations. Early on, the idea of a living wage was contained in labor union contracts and was partially embodied in laws requiring minimum wages or "prevailing wages" for some government contractors, as well as in Social Security, Medicare, and other components of a "social wage." But after rising steadily through the 1960s, the buying power of the minimum wage stagnated in the 1970s and plummeted in the 1980s, contributing to the dramatic rise in inequality. High unemployment, global competition, and the rise of free market ideology further undercut the living-wage ideal.

The contemporary living-wage movement sprang from several sources. In Baltimore in 1994, Baltimoreans United in Leadership Development (BUILD), an Industrial Areas Foundation affiliate, noticed that many people they served in the food banks they operated in churches worked full time in privatized city jobs that once paid decently. BUILD and the American Federation of State, County and Municipal Employees (AFSCME) thus focused on raising wages for city contractors, partly to discourage privatization based on wage cutting. In Minnesota in 1995, critics of welfare reform linked up with plant-closing opponents to force "corporate welfare" recipients to deliver on promises of good jobs. In Los Angeles, a nonprofit group funded by the Hotel Employees and Restaurant Employees (HERE) union defended unionized airport employees who lost their jobs when new minimum-wage firms won the contracts. And, after securing a mandate that city-subsidized businesses turn first to hiring halls in low-income Boston neighborhoods, the Association of Community Organizations for Reform Now (ACORN) turned its attention to winning a living wage from both city contractors and recipients of government subsidies or tax abatements.

If there is a common theme to these efforts, it is the idea that public money should not be used, directly or indirectly, to create jobs that leave workers and their families in poverty. This is a partly moral argument. But it's also an argument for economic fairness: When businesses pay workers poorly, local taxpayers are forced to pick up the slack. Taxpayers end up subsidizing the companies by paying for what the companies will not: workers' unreimbursed medical care, public-hospital visits, food stamps, tax credits, and the social costs of poverty and inequality. Why should businesses be allowed to slough off these costs onto taxpayers? And if taxpayers are ultimately paying the wages of contract employees anyway, why not simply pay the employees a living wage directly?

By focusing criticism on how government is often responsible for the poverty of working people, living-wage campaigns gain moral urgency and strong public support, especially in cities with labor and liberal traditions. But mayors (including many Democrats) and local businesses (especially restaurant owners and other low-wage employers) have put up fights that range from halfhearted to ham-fisted, raising the usual charges against the minimum wage—that it will kill jobs the poor need and benefit workers whose families aren't poor. In many cases, mayors have divided potential allies by using nonprofit human-service contractors—who worry they won't get reimbursed fast enough for the higher wages—as a cover when attacking the living wage.

Most living-wage studies have been prospective estimates of impacts, but the few follow-up studies, including two in Baltimore and San Jose, suggest minimal impact on city budgets. For example, although a few contracts—such as some janitor services—rose sharply, the overall cost of contracted services after the Baltimore ordinance rose less than the rate of inflation. In part, the laws have had modest budget impacts because so few workers have been affected—only about 1,500 in Baltimore, a result exacerbated in many places by poor enforcement and lags in rebidding of contracts. But researchers also conclude that as worker turnover declined and morale improved in response to the wage increase, productivity probably increased. Contractor profit margins may also have been trimmed.

Such results have left living-wage advocates in the peculiar position of arguing that their proposals won't break city budgets because relatively few workers are helped. But advocates now seem more willing to argue that big living-wage increases for more workers are legitimate, even if the city must pay more. For example, the San Francisco coalition admits that its broad coverage of workers in businesses with city contracts could raise annual expenses by $42 million—an amount that the coalition points out is less than the city's budget surplus. After starting with living-wage standards that couldn't even lift a family out of poverty, the movement has increasingly tried to take a bigger bite. "The biggest mistake we made in Los Angeles was that we pegged [the living-wage rate] too low," concludes Jackie Goldberg, who leads the living-wage movement on the L.A. city council.

The Case for Living Wage

Conventional economists typically say that minimum-wage hikes reduce employment, hurting the poor who lose jobs. But in 1994, economists David Card and Alan B. Krueger, after comparing what happened to fast-food businesses in New Jersey and Pennsylvania when New Jersey increased its minimum wage, determined that employment actually went up slightly in New Jersey after the wage hike, in part because employers could fill vacancies more quickly. In a recent paper, Card and Krueger analyzed new data from both the original time period and beyond, including effects of the 1996 federal minimum-wage increase, and reanalyzed the data of critics who claimed New Jersey suffered job losses. They confirmed their original results, concluding that "modest changes in the minimum wage have little systematic effect on employment." Employers compensate for higher wages by managing better, reducing other costs, saving on turnover and recruitment expenses, and gaining productivity from a more motivated workforce. Sometimes these improvements even boost output and employment.

Living-wage laws are in fact even less likely than a minimum-wage increase to lead to unemployment: The city's demand for services is relatively fixed, and some increased costs can be passed from businesses to the municipal government. (For example, Los Angeles law fully compensates any day-care increases to encourage better child care.) Also, contractors can't flee, and businesses leasing city lands are likely stuck in those locations. Businesses, of course, object to having their subsidies tied to living-wage requirements. But ACORN National Living Wage Director Jen Kern has a simple response: "It's not a free market when you're using tax dollars. There's an easy way out: Don't ask for tax dollars."

Contrary to critics' assertions, beneficiaries of broad-based minimum-wage hikes are more likely to be women from poor families—contributing half or more of their family income—than they are to be teenagers from middle-class families working to pay for concert tickets. And living-wage ordinances target poverty even more effectively. Even Michigan State University economist David Neumark, a critic of Card and Krueger who claims that minimum-wage increases reduce employment and increase poverty, concedes that "living-wage increases are associated with small reductions in poverty."

Still, living-wage increases are imperfect solutions to poverty, because as wages go up, government subsidies like food stamps and the Earned Income Tax Credit (EITC) go down. Thus, the net gain in disposable income for workers could be well under half of the apparent living-wage increase, according to an analysis by Robert Pollin and Stephanie Luce, co-authors of *The Living Wage: Building a Fair Economy*. Also, a living-wage ordinance, of course, doesn't benefit people who don't have jobs. Even when living-wage laws do cover part-time workers, a living wage covering limited work hours does not yield a living income.

But while the living-wage movement offers something narrower—and thus politically more viable—than a substantial minimum-wage increase across the board, in some ways it is much more ambitious. Rhetorically it establishes a new rationale for a wage floor—the minimum a family needs in order to live reasonably well—that can inspire political and union demands. But it also sets a new standard for economic development—good jobs, not just any jobs—and corporate accountability. Many living-wage ordinances are designed both to discourage wage cutting and labor degradation and to encourage unionization and "high road" business strategies. Ultimately the movement aims to win greater power for workers—especially low-income workers, on the job and in politics—not just a wage hike.

Living Success Stories

The most ambitious ordinances protect workers' rights in various ways. For example, some ordinances—such as those in Los Angeles and San Jose—require any business that wins a new contract to retain previous employees for at least a few months, protecting workers from churning of contractors. Others prohibit retaliation against workers who demand a living wage, giving local government a tool to protect workers who are organizing a union from being fired. Several cities give preference to developers or "responsible contractors" who will be neutral in organizing drives, and recognize unions simply by checking signed union cards. Pittsburgh and Berkeley organizers hope to prohibit use of city funds for anti-union activity.

The Los Angeles campaign has from the beginning tried to strengthen the hand of workers by using the living-wage ordinance as leverage over businesses bidding for contracts and subsidies. The coalition used the ordinance as an entry point for negotiations with developers of a commercial complex that will be home to the Academy Awards, ultimately winning commitment to union neutrality and a card check, and giving HERE its first new Los Angeles hotel victory in many years. The ordinance has boosted unionization at the Staples Center and the Los Angeles Airport, and the movement has created a new religious coalition, Clergy and Laity United for Economic Justice, which has played a key role in support of organizing drives and contract fights.

The Los Angeles living-wage coalition, working with unions and community allies, has used the living-wage ordinance in these cases to intervene in public decisions about contracts and concessions, supporting businesses that will be less antagonistic toward unions. The openings for unionization are won through political mobilization, but the living-wage law gives the community an opportunity to apply pressure. For example, when a concessionaire at the Los Angeles Airport aggressively opposed unionization, the coalition trained workers about the living-wage ordinance. The workers, in turn, went on to file more than three dozen complaints, prompting a city investigation and potential loss of the concession. The business resolved the problems, and the union won representation. "If we just cared about raising wages, we'd concentrate on raising the minimum wage," says Madeline Janis-

Aparicio, director of the living-wage coalition and the Los Angeles Alliance for a New Economy. "But we want to build a movement from the ground up that empowers working people. So the best way to do that is build their unions. Living-wage legislation is a great tool with a really serious program for doing that."

Now the coalition, working with HERE and Santa Monicans for Responsible Tourism (SMART), which helped successfully fight decertification of the union at a local hotel, is promoting one of the most innovative living-wage ordinances. Santa Monica's "coastal zone," near the ocean, is flush with extremely lucrative hotels that pay very low wages, while the zone has benefited from city beachfront and downtown investments. The coalition wants to require businesses in this zone to pay a living wage and refrain from retaliating against workers who organize to win it. At the same time, HERE is counting on support from SMART in its new drive to organize the hotels. The hotels, deceitfully calling themselves Santa Monicans for a Living Wage, have fought back with an initiative that would cover only about 250 city contract workers and would nullify any other living-wage ordinance passed by the city council. Although a few state legislatures have tried to prohibit cities from adopting living-wage ordinances, the Santa Monica hotels' novel strategy acknowledges the popular appeal of the living-wage idea. "The living-wage campaign has developed a whole consciousness about the status of low-wage workers that hadn't existed before," says HERE organizer and SMART activist Vivian Rothstein.

Baltimore's pioneering campaign spawned the Solidarity Sponsoring Committee, an unorthodox AFSCME local that has a reliable base of 500 members. The local has fought to expand living-wage coverage and regulate exploitative lending and currency-exchange operations. It has established a workers' cooperative, which trains members and places them in temporary catering, construction, janitorial, and clerical jobs, and which can—unlike a commercial employment firm—share its profits with workers and therefore pay them more, typically $8 to $14 an hour. Living-wage campaigns elsewhere have also gone beyond support for union-recognition campaigns to represent workfare recipients, organize part-timers, and press for reform of health care, unemployment insurance, and welfare policies, including a new national campaign to deal with the aftermath of federal welfare reform.

Living-wage advocates in Berkeley and Oakland, California, integrate union organizing and a high-wage economic development strategy into their campaign. After winning an ordinance covering about 300 workers for the city of Oakland, they now have their sights on legislation that would affect 3,000 low-wage workers under the jurisdiction of the Port of Oakland, including the airport and nearby tourist businesses. (Typically local campaigns have to fight for living-wage ordinances for each governmental unit or public authority separately.) HERE, backed by the East Bay Alliance for a Sustainable Economy (EBASE), an outgrowth of the living-wage campaign, pressured a new hotel in Oakland to comply with the ordinance, remain neutral, and abide by a card check in the current organizing drive. Jim DuPont, HERE's local president, thinks that the law will help the union organize not only prime employers, like hotels, but also their contractors, and that it will help raise the standard for other low-wage workers. "I view the living wage as a battle cry for what we need to do in our contracts," he says. "It creates a movement. . . . It's much more than a technical tool if we use it right."

Living-wage campaigns often merge with a parallel movement to make businesses that receive subsidies and tax breaks more publicly accountable. "We're trying to influence economic development and what kinds of business we encourage," says Amaha Kassa, lead organizer of EBASE. "The living-wage tool itself is a substantial lever in redevelopment policy." For example, Oakland abandoned a city-subsidized retail project because tenants wouldn't agree to pay a living wage; the city replaced it with a telecommunications company that would pay living wages and not require a subsidy. There are at least sixty-seven local or state laws that link economic development aid to guarantees of good jobs, including sixteen that specify a living wage, according to Greg Leroy, director of Good Jobs First. "Officials are tired of creating bad jobs," Leroy says. "They don't want to subsidize bottom feeders."

From its relatively narrow origin, the living-wage movement is expanding. Not only do victories in central cities typically inspire campaigns in surrounding municipalities, but the ideas are creeping into state and even federal politics, as demonstrated by the planned introduction this year of separate bills in the House and Senate requiring federal service contractors to pay $8.20 an hour, essentially raising the floor of the "prevailing wage" already required by law. (The impact would be much more dramatic if the federal government also required every human-service provider reimbursed by federal funds—including hospitals, schools, day-care centers, and Head Start programs—to pay all their workers a living wage.)

The living-wage movement is also transforming local politics. Living-wage campaigns propelled movement leaders to the city council in Chicago and San Jose, and both unions and community groups have made support for a living wage a condition for endorsing candidates in several cities. In an unusual tactic, unions in Detroit put a living-wage referendum on the ballot to boost turnout for labor-endorsed candidates. As a result of such campaigns, "no candidate, national or local, can avoid talking about living wages or living-wage jobs," says Keith

Kelleher, a Service Employees union organizer and Chicago campaign leader. "It's changed the political vernacular."

Despite its limitations, the movement has great potential to expand to thousands of new political jurisdictions and to set standards for any business that benefits from public spending. More important, the movement can create a political climate that raises expectations about jobs and incomes, and that supports unionization. Requiring a living wage is particularly important in our political culture, with its emphasis on people working to support themselves, says Robert Pollin in *The Living Wage,* because "it addresses the issue [of inequality] in a way that makes people feel comfortable, that is, giving people a chance to make a living when they show up at a job." The living-wage movement's impact is most likely to spread, however, if unemployment stays low: The tightened labor market of the 1990s has likely been critical to the success of the movement so far. Even under ideal economic circumstances, however, substantially reducing income inequality will require more than even the best current living-wage levels; it will also require universal health care, child care, earned income tax credits, housing subsidies, lifelong education, and other social wages.

The living-wage movement has succeeded so far because it is a broad coalition. But as the movement grows more ambitious, tackling state and federal policies, it will need more coherence. The labor movement can provide some of that organization. Thus far, however, the labor movement nationally has not made building living-wage campaigns a top priority, even though the movement reinforces labor's core messages and provides an opportunity to build broader alliances. If unions hope to organize low-wage workers, coalitions built around the living-wage movement will be invaluable.

Useful as the living-wage ordinances may be in their own right, most organizers see them as a tool for building a social-justice move-ment to challenge economic inequality and give workers more power. "As important as the policies we pass are the coalitions we build," says Oakland organizer Kassa. "The coalition will outlast any policy if we do our job right."

Ladders to a Better Life

The Role of Career-Ladder Strategies in Making Work Pay

JOAN FITZGERALD AND
VIRGINIA CARLSON

One promising strategy for rewarding work seeks to create career ladders to enable low-wage workers to advance through a progression of higher-skilled and better-paid jobs. This approach requires several elements. Employers need to become more explicit about how they structure jobs and routes to career advancement. Workers need access to job-specific training. Institutionally, this endeavor usually requires both an intermediary, such as a community college or a union, and a supportive government strategy to fund and connect all the elements. Even so, many low-wage jobs do not logically lead to higher-paid ones, and a career-ladder strategy is a complement to, not a substitute for, better pay, professionalization, and security throughout the job chain.

Most career-ladder programs are organized by industrial sectors or clusters of occupations. For example, in Chicago, a community organization, Bethel New Life, is trying to move women who work as certified nursing assistants into jobs as licensed practical nurses (LPNs) or, eventually, registered nurses (RNs). In the Seattle area, Shoreline Community College moves welfare recipients from entry-level positions to increasingly better jobs in four occupational clusters. The Milwaukee Graphic Arts Institute's Printing Connections program trains nontraditional recruits, such as women coming off welfare, for work in the printing industry, which then has its own internal ladders to skilled trades.

In our examination of career-ladder strategies, we've found some heartening success stories but also a good deal of lingering resistance. Most people, after all, stay in the same occupation and often the same job for a fairly long time. The economy is continuing to produce many millions of jobs such as nurse's aide, janitor, retail salesclerk, mailroom worker, and others that need to pay better wages in their own right as well as being restructured as springboards to something better. Still, the career-ladder approach could be broadly beneficial if its potential were maximized. Our exploration of career-ladder programs in several states and industries raises these questions:

What kinds of intermediaries or sponsors work best?

What overall labor-market strategy serves as a conductive policy environment?

What financial resources are needed?

How does the career-ladder approach interact with welfare reform?

How important are unions?

How resistant are employers (and, in some cases, other employees)?

What prevents low-wage workers from taking advantage of available training programs?

How do downsizing and outsourcing constrain career ladders?

Unwilling Employers, Inexperienced Workers

Career-ladder strategies depend on employers being willing to create jobs with advancement potential and to think explicitly about the company's internal labor market. But, in many cases, there is employer resistance. Many companies have downsized their labor force and outsourced their work, thus changing the nature of the ladder—the first rung is now higher, and some rungs along the way up may be missing. Some employers simply find it more cost-effective to rely on a casual, high-turnover, low-wage workforce, and naturally resist making their internal labor market more explicit and better structured. The makeup of the workforce trying to climb the ladder is increasingly darker and more female than companies are used to seeing, and many firms are not programmed to offer nontraditional ladders to women and minorities. Some industries, such as printing and metalworking, are dominated by small firms with short ladders, and in the absence of deliberate strategies, it may be difficult to advance by moving among firms. And then there's the issue of maintaining status within some occupations. Registered nurses, for example, justifiably proud that their profession requires a college degree, may resist efforts to make the RN credential more accessible to experienced health workers via on-the-job training—again, keeping that first rung high.

There are also obstacles from the would-be climbers themselves. To attach oneself to the labor market and commit to advancement on the job means trade-offs and adjustments in other areas of life. Many people coming off welfare or otherwise working full time for the first time find these adjustments difficult. There are real obstacles to continuing education: parenting responsibilities, financial costs, child-care arrangements, and a general scarcity of time. Unless time off and financial subsidies are available for training, the next rung may be out of reach. This same cluster of family demands, transportation problems, and so on may create a spotty work history, which then leads the employer to be skeptical of whether the worker belongs on a ladder to a better job. Race and gender issues play a role here on both the employer and employee sides. It may be difficult for workers to find mentors or models, formal or informal, to whom they can look and say, "Well, if they made it, so can I."

Finally, there are public-policy obstacles. Despite several generations of labor market policy, most states and cities have not structured their programs to maximize the potential of career ladders. Yet good programs have managed to overcome these obstacles and demonstrate real success.

Health Care Ladders

Health care is seemingly an ideal sector to pursue a career-ladder strategy. It has lots of entry-level and paraprofessional positions, and demand will continue to grow with the aging of the population, the growth of community-based care, and the downsizing of hospital care. But are there career ladders for, say, dietary aides or certified nursing assistants (CNAs)? It depends. Three approaches are noteworthy: moving people into progressively better-paying occupations that require more education or training, increasing the pay and professionalization of jobs that currently exist, and creating tiers within occupations that offer pay increases.

Bethel New Life, a church-based community development corporation on Chicago's West Side, started the Health Care Career Ladder project to provide training and support services for low-income women in health-care occupations. Bethel staff hoped to start trainees in home health aide skills, then move them to CNA, then to LPN, RN, or other allied health professions such as respiratory therapist, lab technician, or phlebotomist.

Of the 150 participants who began as home health aides in the past three years, ninety-five (63 percent) have completed CNA training, but only five are enrolled in community college RN programs, and to date none has moved into other better-paying technical jobs such as phlebotomist. Of the ninety-five, fifty-nine are still working, mostly in nursing homes, and are earning an average hourly wage of $7.20. While this is a big gain over the $5.40 they made as home health aides, it's not yet a living wage. Most of the women find the transition to employment difficult and need at least six weeks to adjust to employment before attempting to enroll in the CNA program while working. CNA seems more a stopping point than a starting point, as other programs take a long time to complete on top of a full-time job. A few CNAs have had supervisory and quality-control tasks added to their jobs, which have raised their hourly wage, but only by 30 to 50 cents an hour. Without undertaking the LPN or RN training, their only avenue for wage enhancement is moving from nursing homes to hospitals, where wages tend to be higher. Two participants working as CNAs in hospitals are now earning $11 an hour.

Bethel's experience is not unique. The Annie E. Casey Foundation's $30 million Jobs Initiative program, which began in 1995, reports success stories in connecting low-income communities to job opportunities in office occupations, construction, and manufacturing. But organizations in Seattle and Denver participating in the Casey Jobs Initiative have had difficulty extracting commitments from the health-care industry to structure ladders for advancement.

The National Network of Career Nursing Assistants tends to be skeptical of career ladders and focuses instead on improving recognition, pay, quality of training, and professionalization generally. Director Genevieve Gipson sees high turnover as a function of the low wages, lack of benefits, unreasonable work demands, lack of advancement opportunities, and lack of respect given to the job. She notes that it is impossible for CNAs to perform their five main responsibilities—assisting with bathing, eating, eliminating, ambulating, dressing—for up to twenty patients per shift. The stress of overwork is a major factor in job dissatisfaction. Her study of job leavers found that many are good workers and like the job but can't earn a sufficient income to support their families as CNAs; that what nurse's assistants want most is the opportunity for professional growth and advancement within their present occupation. The majority who have five or more years of seniority aren't interested in other jobs. What they want is pay raises as they achieve higher levels of competency. What they get is higher expectations without pay raises. Some CNAs specialize in more intensive-care areas, such as oncology or restorative care, but typically there are neither pay raises associated with these specializations nor recognition that they even are specializations. Another unrecognized and uncompensated specialization of more experienced CNAs is helping with on-the-job training of entry-level workers. But experienced workers are not explicitly trained for this role, nor are they provided a support system for doing it.

The network and the Service Employees International Union (SEIU) are trying to get specializations and the training role recognized as job titles, with training and higher pay associated with them. Given the limited success of community-based career-ladder programs in health-care occupations, improving the working conditions and pay of CNAs might be more effective than focusing on job ladders.

One well-known program that takes this approach is Cooperative Home Care Associates (CHCA), founded in 1985 in the South Bronx. CHCA is a worker cooperative that provides high-quality workers to health-care agencies. It has convinced home health-care agencies of the advantages of paying higher wages for better-trained employees. The program provides considerably more training than the two-week minimum federal requirement and three-week requirement in the state of New York. The entry-level program includes four weeks of on-site classroom training followed by ninety days of on-the-job training. While the industry is characterized by part-time work and low wages, CHCA's employees are paid starting hourly wages between $7 and $8. Approximately 70 percent are employed full time. At CHCA, full-time employees are eligible for health insurance, paid vacation, and sick days as well as life insurance.

There are two opportunities for job upgrading at CHCA. First, employees are encouraged to apply for administrative jobs. Of the thirty-five current administrative staffers, twelve were former home health aides. Second, employees are encouraged to continue their education. CHCA partners with Bronx College in offering home-care classes through which students can earn up to twelve credits. A third program now being developed will offer home health aides additional training and wages to work with disabled people. CHCA employs 500 in the Bronx, 85 percent of whom were receiving some form of public assistance upon entering the program. CHCA has far less turnover—about 18 percent annually—than most agencies that provide nurse's aides, because the job is normalized and professionalized rather than treated as cheap, casual labor.

The Crucial Role of Unions

Notwithstanding the appeal of the co-op model, the single most effective strategy both for improving pay and working conditions and for creating career ladders for paraprofessional health workers is unionization. The average hourly wage for a union nursing assistant is $10.17, while the average nonunion assistant earns $8.55. Just being unionized, with no career ladders, improves average wages by almost 20 percent. And many SEIU union locals that represent health-care workers have negotiated career ladders into their contracts. Nancy Mills, director of the AFL-CIO Center for Workplace Democracy, notes that there are hundreds of career-ladder programs throughout the country negotiated by union locals.

For example, the Cape Cod Hospital career-ladder program was created through an agreement with SEIU Local 767. The program offers classes for union members in nonprofessional occupations such as housekeeper or dietary assistant. The program also represents a commitment to promoting from within. About 80 percent of all job openings in the hospital are promotions from lower positions.

Working with the joint labor-management committee to develop the courses has helped human-resource staff to reevaluate the precise skill requirements of occupations. Two courses that underpin any further training, medical terminology and computer data entry, are taught on site by community college staff. The program is designed to make continuing education as easy as possible. Courses are offered between shifts—meaning that employees can quit one hour early or start one hour later to take a class offered on site. Thus, the hospital and the employee each donate an hour to continuing education. This deal is only available for courses offered on site, which are basic education classes. There is a $25 fee for courses, which is refunded on completion of the course.

The hospital also offers traineeships, aimed mainly at teaching workers how to perform additional procedures within an occupation. For example, a licensed and registered X-ray technician can learn how to do CT scans on the job. Then, when that position becomes vacant, the employee becomes eligible to advance into it. There is a tuition-reimbursement program for continuing education off site. The hospital and union jointly publish an annual job-ladders book for employees. The book lists all jobs and their requirements. Workers can find their existing jobs and identify the exact requirements of another job, including classes, degrees, or certificates. Further, the book lists the assistance available, through the hospital or elsewhere, to complete the courses needed.

The job-ladder program was negotiated between the hospital and the union local. Both consider it a win-win proposition. The union ensures opportunities for its members, and the hospital reduces turnover and saves money in outside training and recruiting since most positions are filled from within. Hospital officials are very enthusiastic about the program.

Good as the program is, the most frequent job advancement is from housekeeping to secretarial or clerical support staff. But unionization makes even these jobs relatively well-paying. Most nonprofessionals at the hospital start at $10.19 per hour with full benefits. CNAs with no experience start at $11.37 an hour and can advance to $15.91. But few CNAs advance to other positions. Employee relations manager Arthur LaChance cites the difficulty of holding down a full-time job while raising a family as a major barrier to advancement. Kim Evon, a staff representative at Local 767, notes that some CNAs do not want to move to RN, but do take advantage of programs in occupations such as radiation technician or billing clerk.

In Philadelphia, the American Federation of State, County and Municipal Employees (AFSCME) District 1199C Training and Upgrading Fund offers one solution for moving CNAs into LPN positions. The fund is a trust negotiated between the union local and the hospitals, nursing homes, and other health-care facilities, to which management contributes 1.5 percent of gross payroll. It serves over 10,000 workers annually through various training programs, counseling, placement, certification testing, and workshops. The fund just opened a school of practical nursing that is approved by the Pennsylvania Board of Nursing. Because the union receives grants from the Department of Labor and other government funding sources and foundations, it can make the program available to community residents as well as union members.

The first LPN class of thirty-one students started in March 1999. The program extends the full-time, yearlong course to eighteen months because it is offered on evenings and weekends to accommodate work schedules. Tuition is $7,100. Union members may apply for tuition reimbursement, leaves of absence with stipends, and other forms of assistance. Over the next two years, eighty scholarships will be available to RN and LPN students through a U.S. Department of Labor H1-B grant and employer matches. Welfare-to-work program community members are also eligible for scholarships.

Students who want to advance, but don't have the math or English skills, have several options. The state funds a free course for applicants to prepare for the LPN admission test. The union fund offers two levels of prenursing prep that combine English, math, and anatomy. This has been an important vehicle for recruiting people who may not qualify initially. Half the students in the first class had to take at least one of the basic education or prenursing courses. According to Cheryl Feldman, coordinator of the fund's Learning Center, the Philadelphia area has a shortage of LPNs, so graduates are practically guaranteed a job. Union CNAs make $13 an hour in hospitals and $8 to $10 an hour in nursing homes. Working as LPNs, they would make over $20 an hour.

In addition, the training fund encourages entry-level workers to advance by offering other courses on site and providing scholarships of $10,000 with leaves of absence and stipends to union members for completing college and vocational school courses. Occupations include therapeutic support service aide, claims processing clerk, and mental health/mental retardation worker.

Nontraditional Workers in Printing Trades

A whole other strategy is to help nontraditional applicants overcome barriers to highly paid occupations that have well-established career ladders within or among employers. This is typical of the skilled, and highly unionized, trades. For most of the skilled trades, the attraction is less the career ladder than the high wages. Printing, as a very long established trade, offers a richer set of career ladders than other trades where one is either an apprentice or a journeyman.

Mary Roberts (not her real name), thirty-one, has lived in Milwaukee for fifteen years and has had several short-term jobs. With three school-age children, she left a stint on a second-shift office cleaning-crew about six months ago, when her nine-year-old fell behind in school because Roberts was not around at night to help with homework. She supports herself with a combination of public assistance, some child support, and occasional gifts from family members. But when the youngest started school full time last fall, she decided to find a job with career prospects. Her caseworker at the local job center referred her to a program at the Milwaukee Graphic Arts Institute called Printing Connections for entry-level printing-industry training. The institute also does incumbent worker training and helps guide entry-level workers along a career path once they have finished the Connections training and have gotten a job.

Connections incorporates much of what is considered the best practice in job training. It has strong employer partnerships, with several companies committed to hiring graduates of each training class. Even so, there has been relatively little mobility within the printing trades to date. Of the 110 total placements since August 1997, eighty-eight workers were working as of December 1999, sixty for printing companies. But just seven have risen up the career ladder, and seventeen have experienced wage gains. (Only twelve received training in late 1999.) As a Connections staffperson explains, "Advancement means a more complex network of move-ups from company to company. This is actually the way most printers have developed their careers—bouncing from one shop to a better shop, et cetera, until they land the best-skilled job. Only a few shops offer a cradle-to-grave type of career growth."

Compounding the problem are occupational and technological changes. Computerization has brought an explosion of printed material. Computers have eliminated several specialties but also have increased the volume of printed matter dramatically. The effect on occupational ladders has been multifaceted. On the one hand, relatively more workers are needed in the bindery and finishing areas, which tend to be lower skilled, but more sophisticated workers are needed in the press and prepress areas. It is not that "middle" occupations or career ladders have disappeared. Rather, lower-skilled jobs (stitching, cutting, folding, and so on) have increased at a faster rate than higher-skilled ones such as press operator.

Also, employers are struggling to understand a new workforce that is usually not male and not white. As Renee Zakhar, a recruiter for Connections, explains, "One of the keys here is to get at the fact that the career paths in printing were defined for the 1940s and 1950s. Young boys followed their dads or uncles to work, spent years working their way up, got the inside scoop from their family and peers. Today's workforce comes from a different background, with and without different skills and issues, including family responsibilities."

Although many of these new workers are not yet advancing, they are at least keeping their jobs at a higher rate than people in many other skills training programs. In large part, this is due to the effort that Connections staff have put into building and maintaining relationships. Project staff have to find potential trainees, get companies on board, secure funding streams, and coordinate the myriad details that such undertakings require. They serve as personal intermediaries between the employees and the employers, each of whom is struggling to understand the other and the new workforce situation they face.

The Two Worlds of Banking

A number of community colleges and community organizations offer bank teller training as part of their welfare-to-work programs. The experience of a teller training program developed at Wright College, one of Chicago's city colleges, suggests that there are great obstacles but also windows of opportunity in creating banking career ladders for entry-level workers.

Developed in 1996, Bank Tellers and Beyond devised a comprehensive thirteen-week occupations program that prepares students with eighth-grade reading and math levels for teller jobs paying between $8 and $11.50 per hour. The college personnel enlisted a consortium of banks to identify needed competencies and build a curriculum. Banking professionals are used as instructors. Students must have a high school diploma or be enrolled in a GED program. The program starts with general "soft" employment skills (employability, intensive customer service, communications, math for banking), then moves on to basic bank operations and regulations, ten-key pad proficiency, cash handling, process and procedures, and computer literacy. The bank partners assist in student selection using a screening instrument developed with the college to provide some instructors for classroom teaching, and conduct mock interviews. Some of the banks are assisting with scholarship funds for needy students. In the early years of the course, graduates attended a monthly seminar after placement for assessing their work performance, learning stress management techniques, and building job-keeping skills.

The program had all the right stuff—good curriculum, employer involvement, support services, and postplacement follow-up—yet the retention rate of early graduates at most banks was no higher than that of those hired "off the street." Few tellers advanced. The banks expressed little interest in the college developing further courses to build skills for advancement.

Why? Because the teller position has never been a reliable route upward. For centuries, bankers divided their workers into a clerical force that included tellers and higher-paid "platform" positions. And in the past fifteen years, direct depositing, telephone banking, the Internet, and, most significantly, automated teller machines (ATMs) have dramatically restructured the job of teller—but for the most part have not upgraded it.

Slightly over half of all bank transactions still take place at the teller window. ATMs, however, have changed the nature of what tellers do. In some banks, the use of ATMs for routine banking transactions has led to the upgrading of teller positions. More frequently, though, tellers still conduct only routine transactions, while customer-service representatives and officers, typically college graduates, open new accounts and sell bank products such as loans and CDs. The percentage of banking jobs accounted for by sales workers nearly doubled between 1983–85 and 1993–95.

With the emphasis on sales, many banks changed telling from a predominantly full-time position to a part-time and peak-time job with even less opportunity for moving into better or full-time positions. We interviewed six human resource directors at six large Chicago banks, who told us that teller turnover rates were between 60 and 80 percent. As a result, banks are always looking for tellers. Two directors mentioned that the increase in part-time and peak-time scheduling has reduced employee loyalty, particularly in banks that make it clear to prospective employees that neither part-time nor peak-time jobs are stepping-stones to full-time positions. Thus, many entry-level employees see their position as temporary or transitional and leave as soon as another opportunity emerges. Banks have adapted to high turnover by hiring college or high school students, knowing that they will not stay on after graduation. Treating tellers as casual labor seems more cost-effective to managers than making the teller position a permanent first rung on a career ladder.

There are exceptions, however. Some banks are recognizing that tellers are the front line for customer contact. Laura O'Kuly, who has hired and trained entry-level workers for customer services and tellers for the First National Bank of Chicago (now merged with Bank One), points out that as customers used to ATMs and online banking are more savvy, they no longer confront tellers or customer-service representatives with basic questions like "What's my balance?" By the time they get to a frontline, live person, they have more sophisticated questions, such as "How did you calculate my finance charge?" O'Kuly maintains that banks have historically ignored skills-upgrading of these customer-line functions. But recently First Chicago and other banks have recognized the value of investing more in their frontline workforce, both in training and in offering full-time employment.

According to Nancy Bellew, at Bank Tellers and Beyond, the program has evolved into a unique training endeavor that emphasizes skill sets needed by the new customer-service-oriented tellers. The post-placement seminar has evolved into an ongoing mentoring program. Citibank now hires former welfare recipients trained by the program at starting salaries of $22,000 and has invested $20,000 in scholarships; other banks are discussing having the program develop skills-upgrading courses. These developments have already begun to improve retention rates and job satisfaction. Even so, banking has a long way to go before it becomes a model industry for career ladders.

The Community College as Intermediary

Shoreline Community College in Seattle is one of the few community colleges integrating career ladders into its welfare-to-work programs. The Job Ladder Partnership brings Shoreline and six other community or technical colleges together with employers to create work and learning pathways in four occupational clusters: manufacturing, customer relations, health services, and information technology.

Funding for the program is the result of the commitment of governor Gary Locke to focus welfare reform on moving people out of poverty and not just off welfare. Locke sees the state's community college system as essential in accomplishing this goal. To realize it, the state of Washington made an initial transfer of $17 million from the Department of Social and Health Services to the State Board for Community and Technical Colleges in 1998. The funds were earmarked for developing programs to promote job advancement and wage progression. In 1999 an additional $20 million was allocated for the programs.

Dr. Holly Moore, vice president for workforce and economic development at Shoreline, organized a partnership of the six community colleges serving the suburban parts of the county to work together on developing a coordinated strategy for using the new funds. Although each college develops its own programs, the colleges share business partners and stagger offerings. One college may offer a course in the evenings if another is offering it during the day. Elsewhere, the network of community colleges is often fragmented and competitive.

A guiding principle of Shoreline's Job Ladder Partnership is to combine education and work as much as possible. Students go through an initial assessment and are then placed in the pre-employment program, work, remedial classes, or English as a Second Language classes. As soon as students have enough skills to begin an entry-level job in one of the chosen sectors, they have to combine work and continuing education. Students develop a career plan early on and work with a counselor to keep moving ahead on their career goals.

The career ladders are not necessarily rungs within a single business or even a sector. Rather, they are based on clusters of skills that could prepare students for any number of occupations.

The career pathways depicted identify many possibilities for advancement. A retention specialist, who serves as a liaison between students and employers, works with students in choosing one of the paths. A computerized career-planning tool, the Career Pathway Passport, is being developed. The interactive program will allow students, working with their retention specialist, to develop career plans and document their progress. The passport will have two databases—one listing available jobs in the four career pathways offered by the employer partners; another containing the education programs offered by the six partner colleges in these fields, with contact names listed.

Health Services

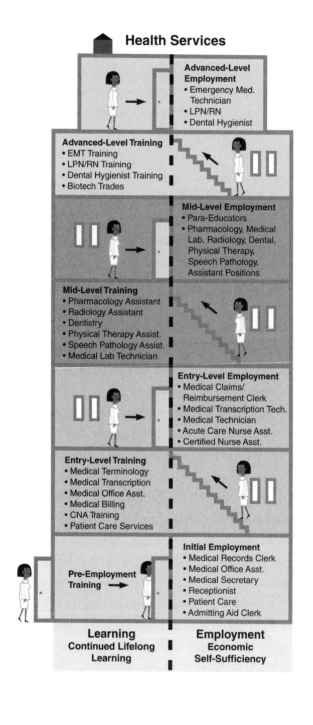

Advanced-Level Employment
- Emergency Med. Technician
- LPN/RN
- Dental Hygienist

Advanced-Level Training
- EMT Training
- LPN/RN Training
- Dental Hygienist Training
- Biotech Trades

Mid-Level Employment
- Para-Educators
- Pharmacology, Medical Lab, Radiology, Dental, Physical Therapy, Speech Pathology, Assistant Positions

Mid-Level Training
- Pharmacology Assistant
- Radiology Assistant
- Dentistry
- Physical Therapy Assist.
- Speech Pathology Assist.
- Medical Lab Technician

Entry-Level Employment
- Medical Claims/Reimbursement Clerk
- Medical Transcription Tech.
- Medical Technician
- Acute Care Nurse Asst.
- Certified Nurse Asst.

Entry-Level Training
- Medical Terminology
- Medical Transcription
- Medical Office Asst.
- Medical Billing
- CNA Training
- Patient Care Services

Initial Employment
- Medical Records Clerk
- Medical Office Asst.
- Medical Secretary
- Receptionist
- Patient Care
- Admitting Aid Clerk

Pre-Employment Training →

Learning
Continued Lifelong Learning

Employment
Economic Self-Sufficiency

Customer Relations

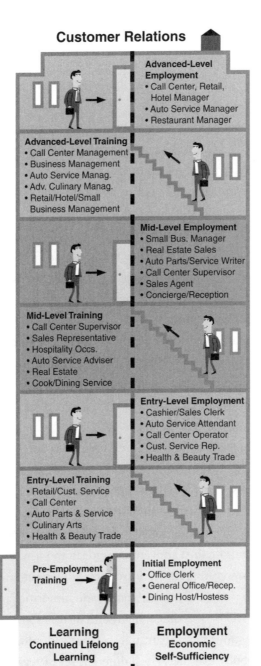

Advanced-Level Employment
- Call Center, Retail, Hotel Manager
- Auto Service Manager
- Restaurant Manager

Advanced-Level Training
- Call Center Management
- Business Management
- Auto Service Manag.
- Adv. Culinary Manag.
- Retail/Hotel/Small Business Management

Mid-Level Employment
- Small Bus. Manager
- Real Estate Sales
- Auto Parts/Service Writer
- Call Center Supervisor
- Sales Agent
- Concierge/Reception

Mid-Level Training
- Call Center Supervisor
- Sales Representative
- Hospitality Occs.
- Auto Service Adviser
- Real Estate
- Cook/Dining Service

Entry-Level Employment
- Cashier/Sales Clerk
- Auto Service Attendant
- Call Center Operator
- Cust. Service Rep.
- Health & Beauty Trade

Entry-Level Training
- Retail/Cust. Service
- Call Center
- Auto Parts & Service
- Culinary Arts
- Health & Beauty Trade

Pre-Employment Training →

Initial Employment
- Office Clerk
- General Office/Recep.
- Dining Host/Hostess

Learning
Continued Lifelong Learning

Employment
Economic Self-Sufficiency

Toward Sturdier Ladders

Our tour of career-ladder strategies suggests several conclusions for policy makers. Ladders will succeed or fail depending on whether these lessons are learned and implemented.

State government policy matters. Washington has facilitated the Job Ladder Partnership at Shoreline Community College in two ways. First, the state earmarked funds from Temporary Assistance for Needy Families (TANF) savings specifically for developing job ladders for low-income workers, while many other states have left hundreds of millions in TANF savings unspent. Second, Washington has been a leader in education reform throughout the 1990s. The secondary and community college systems are moving from diplomas based on seat time to certificates of mastery based on skills. At a time when more and more employers are saying they want skills, not diplomas, this move has given career-ladder programs such as Shoreline's an edge in delivering workers who come on board ready.

Industry structure matters. Some industries don't have viable career ladders. The printing industry is dominated by small firms, so advancements must take place between firms rather than within the same firm, making those steps more difficult. Printing is also, like many manufacturing industries, traditionally male, with both workers and employers struggling against conventional ideas about who "belongs" on the ladder. Despite programs to introduce women into nontraditional and well-paying blue-collar jobs, women and minorities are often skeptical that they will be welcomed; many aim instead for a college degree. As one Connections participant put it, "I walked into the shop, and I didn't see anybody like me." For a different set of reasons, entry-level positions in banking have few career ladders. In both cases, helping people to move up requires more intensive intervention from intermediaries like those described in the Printing Connections and Shoreline job-ladder programs.

Relationships matter. Successful programs have long-term staff members who build and maintain relationships with recruitment sources, employers, and the workers themselves. Nancy Bellew, who has been with the Bank Tellers and Beyond program since its inception, was able to maintain relationships with Chicago banking employers and to devise continuous incremental improvements. Unsuccessful programs invariably have high staff turnover. The corollary is that programs need the long-term funding and institutional support that allow this kind of lengthy programmatic focus.

Unions matter. Unionized workers in entry-level positions, such as janitors or CNAs, earn more and have benefits. Many people in these positions have neither the desire nor the ability to move into more advanced positions. Rather than assuming that everyone wants to engage in lifelong learning, we need policies to ensure that everyone who works should earn a decent wage and have health benefits as well as opportunities to pursue advancement. Unions are our single best bet for making this happen. For those who do choose to advance, some union locals have negotiated upgrade training into their contracts.

Evidence from the Cape Cod Hospital program and the AFSCME District 1199C Training and Upgrading Fund suggests that because union training programs are negotiated directly with employers, they may have an edge over other intermediaries with weaker knowledge of, or leverage on, employers. The long jump from teller to customer-service representative is not surprising, given that banking is almost entirely nonunion.

Mapping matters. Career ladders are not always linear. Cape Cod Hospital, Shoreline, and the Connections project provide employees and students with guidance on exactly what it takes to get from one point to another in a career ladder. This is especially critical when that ladder involves moving from company to company, as in the printing industry.

Family situation matters. Career ladders aren't for everyone. In almost every interview, we were told that for many women it is hard enough to manage full-time work and family responsibilities, let alone fit in continuing education. Recent research by Kathryn Edin and Laura Lein indicates that single mothers making an adequate wage will forgo further time investments in training in order to spend time at home with their children.

Findings from the New Hope welfare-to-work demonstration project in Milwaukee bear this out (see Gordon L. Berlin, "Welfare That Works"). Low-income workers chose time with families over more training or schooling. However, the availability of subsidies also matters and can offset this tension. Cape Cod Hospital's experience suggests that participation in education programs increases when at least some of it is on company time. But perhaps even more important, according to Nancy Mills, national workforce coordinator at the AFL-CIO, is that people are willing to enroll in continuing education only when the connections to a better job and higher pay are guaranteed.

Although some graduates are eager to continue their education while working, others find that the adjustment from not working to going to school, then to employment, is enough of a life change. John Lederer of Shoreline College explains, "When you're dealing with a single parent who has been out of the labor force, going to school is very new, intensive, and stressful. Then they are placed in a job. They have a lot vested in that job. Several students have declined to go back to school right away, telling me that they need to focus on the job if they're going to succeed."

On balance, career ladders are not a magic bullet, but they can be an important part of a national commitment to make work pay. We already know enough, from various experiments, about what works. What is missing is the political will to take full advantage of this approach.

The Other Gender Gap

Why Women Still Fail to Receive Comparable Wages for Comparable Work

NAOMI BARKO

azel Dews is slightly embarrassed when you ask about her salary. She pauses and then confesses that after twenty-five years cleaning the Russell Senate Office Building in Washington five nights a week, she makes barely $22,000 a year. That's not what really bothers her, though. What irks her is that men who do the same job earn $30,000.

The men, she explains, are called "laborers." They can progress five grades. The women, however, are called "custodial workers," which means they can only advance two grades. "But," she protests, "they scrub with a mop and bucket. We scrub with a mop and bucket. They vacuum. We vacuum. They push a trash truck. We push a trash truck. The only thing they do that we don't is run a scrub machine. But that's on wheels, so we could do it too."

Thirty-seven years after the Equal Pay Act of 1963, American women working full time still earn an average of 74 cents for each dollar earned by men, according to a new report published jointly by the AFL-CIO and the Institute for Women's Policy Research (IWPR) in Washington, D.C. This affects all economic classes, but its impact is strongest on lower-income workers: If men and women were paid equally, more than 50 percent of low-income households across the country—dual-earner as well as single-mother—would rise above the poverty line.

New figures challenge the long-heard arguments that women's lower pay results from fewer years in the workforce or time out for childbearing and rearing. The Women's Bureau of the Department of Labor cites a study by the president's Council of Economic Advisers showing that even in light of the vicissitudes of motherhood, 43 percent of the wage gap remains "unexplained," evidently due in large part to discrimination.

The Overview of Salary Surveys, published in 1999 by the National Committee on Pay Equity (NCPE)—a coalition of thirty women's, civil rights, and religious groups—summarized twenty-three surveys of specific salary titles conducted by professional associations and trade magazines. It reported that, for instance, among women engineers—where the salary gap averages 26 percent—women with the same qualifications continue to earn less than men even after they've been in the field for many years (20.4 percent less among women with a B.S. degree and twenty to twenty-four years of experience; 19.2 percent less among women with an M.S. degree and twenty to twenty-four years experience). Yet another study found that women physicians earned less than men in forty-four of forty-five specialties, including obstetrics-gynecology (14 percent less) and pediatrics (15.8 percent less), with lower compensation only partly explainable by hours worked or time spent in the field. And a 1999 report by the American Association of

University Professors found that though women had grown from 23 to 34 percent of faculty since 1975, the salary gap had actually widened in that time period.

But the biggest reason for the pay gap is not discrimination against individual women but rather discrimination against women's occupations. As the percentage of women in an occupation rises, wages tend to fall. More than 55 percent of employed women work in traditional "women's jobs"—librarians, clerical workers, nurses, teachers, and child-care workers. If these women are compared not to male workers but to women with similar education and experience in more gender-balanced occupations, they would earn about 18 percent—or $3,446—more per year, according to the IWPR. (The 8.5 percent of men in these jobs earn an average of $6,259 less per year than men of comparable backgrounds working in "men's" fields.)

Why are "women's jobs" less lucrative? Is a truck driver—who earns an average annual wage of $25,030—really 45 percent more valuable than a child-care worker who may have a four-year degree in early childhood education? Is a beginning engineer really worth between 30 and 70 percent more than a beginning teacher? Rarely, in the almost daily reports of teacher shortages, is it mentioned that the market alone cannot account for the striking disparity between teachers' and other professionals' salaries. No one ever suggests that it might have something to do with the fact that 75 percent of elementary and secondary schoolteachers are women.

In response to these disparities, women are beginning to mobilize. Three years ago, for example, Hazel Dews and 300 of her fellow women custodians joined the American Federation of State, County and Municipal Employees (AFSCME), which, after several futile attempts to negotiate, is now suing Dews's employer, the Architect of the Capitol, for equal pay. Since 1997, as women's membership in the labor movement has mushroomed to 40 percent, the AFL-CIO has conducted two surveys to discover the chief concerns of both union and nonunion working women. "And the runaway answer was equal pay," reports Karen Nussbaum, the director of the AFL-CIO's working women's department. Ninety-four percent of women in both surveys said equal pay was a top concern, and one-third—one-half of African-American women—said they did not have equal pay in their own jobs.

In 1999, calling pay equity a "family issue," the labor movement helped launch equal-pay bills in both houses of Congress and twenty-seven state legislatures. Also last year, as Dews and her co-workers were demonstrating at the Capitol, the Eastman Kodak Company was agreeing to pay $13 million in present and retroactive wages to employees underpaid on the basis of either race or gender. The Massachusetts Institute of Technology, after protests by women faculty, made an unprecedented admission that it had discriminated against women "in salaries, space, awards, resources and response to outside offers."

Moreover, since 1997, the Office of Federal Contract Compliance Programs (OFCCP) has collected $10 million in equal-pay settlements from such corporations as Texaco, US Airways, Pepsi-Cola, the computer manufacturer Gateway, and health insurer Highmark, Inc. At the same time, two major national chains, Home Depot and Publix Supermarkets, agreed to pay more than $80 million each to settle lawsuits based on sex discrimination.

Recently, advocates have arrived at what they believe to be an effective means of generating pay equity—the concept of "comparable worth," which, as the name suggests, requires two people with comparable skills, education, and experience to be paid comparable amounts, even when they're working at two very different jobs. The Xerox Corporation, for example, uses comparable-worth analysis, weighing such factors as education, experience, skill, responsibility, decision making, and discomfort or danger in working conditions, to set salary levels within the country. During the 1980s, some twenty state governments studied the comparable worth of their own employees and made adjustments totaling almost $750 million in increased pay to women. Minnesota, the leader in the field, has made pay-equity adjustments in 1,544 counties and localities.

Perhaps the most dramatic argument for comparable worth, however, was made by a man. In the class-action suit *AFSCME v. Washington State* in 1982, one of the nine named plaintiffs was Milt Tedrow, a licensed practical nurse at Eastern State Hospital in Spokane. Approaching retirement and realizing that his "woman's" job wouldn't give him much of a pension, Tedrow switched to carpentry at the same hospital. To qualify as an LPN, he had needed at least four years of experience, four quarters of schooling, and a license. As a carpenter, he was self-taught, had no paid work experience, and had no need of a license. And yet, when he transferred from the top of the LPN wage scale to the bottom of the carpenter's, his salary jumped more than $200 a month—from $1,614 to $1,826. Why, Tedrow wondered at the time, does the state resent "paying people decently who are taking care of people's bodies, when they'd pay a lot for someone fixing cars or plumbing"?

Since then, the courts have ruled that evidence of unfair salaries is not enough to prove violation of the Equal Pay Act. Plaintiffs must prove that employers intentionally discriminated by lowering women's wages in comparison to men's. But some unions have prevailed on comparable-worth questions by way of negotiations.

For example, Service Employees International Union Local 715, in Santa Clara County, just south of San Francisco, won nearly $30 million for 4,500 county employees, from secretaries to mental-health counselors. A study of some 150 job titles, performed by a consulting firm chosen jointly by the county and the union, showed that underpayment was common in job classes with more than 50 percent minorities, such as licensed vocational nurses and beginning social workers, and that 70 percent of such positions were filled by women. "We worked for at least three years to bring our male members along on this," says Kristy Sermersheim, Local 715's executive secretary. "When the county argued that in order to raise women's wages they'd have to lower men's, we refused to even discuss it. We kept regular pay negotiations completely separate."

Another key to the local's success was the staunch support of allies among local women's groups. "We had fifty-four women's community groups on our side," reports Sermersheim. "The National Organization for Women, the American Association of University Women, the League of Women Voters, the Silicon Valley women engineers. . . ." On the day the county board of supervisors voted on whether to proceed with the study, the local delivered 1,000 pink balloons—symbolizing the pink-collar ghetto—to workplaces around the city. "We had balloons everywhere," recalls Sermersheim. "We had Unitarian women out there singing 'Union Maid.' "

It is this kind of coalition that pay-equity advocates are counting on to push through the equal-pay bills now before state legislatures. Many of the new bills, unlike those passed in the 1980s, would extend comparable worth to private as well as public employees and would specifically extend benefits to minorities. Most are based on the Fair Pay Act designed in consultation with the NCPE—and introduced in Congress in 1999 by two Democrats, Senator Tom Harkin of Iowa and Representative Eleanor Holmes Norton of the District of Columbia. (A more modest Paycheck Fairness Act, backed by the Clinton administration, would toughen the Equal Pay Act of 1963 by removing present caps on damages and making it easier to bring class-action suits.)

So far, the new state bills have met with only modest success. The New Jersey and New Mexico legislatures have voted to study pay equity in both public and private employment, and Vermont's legislature voted to study just state employment. In Maine, where the new welfare laws gave rise to a commission to study poverty among working parents, it was discovered that the state already had a 1965 law on the books that mandated equal pay for both public and private employees and that specifically mentioned comparable worth. The state is now studying ways to put the law into effect.

Efforts like these have raised opposition from business and conservative groups. Economist Diana Furchgott-Roth, a resident fellow at the American Enterprise Institute who recently represented business at an NCPE forum, supports "equal pay for equal work" but claims that comparable worth causes labor shortages because men refuse to take jobs where their wages will be tied to women's. "How can a government bureaucrat calculate if a secretary is worth the same as a truck driver, or a nurse as an oil driller?"

In Ontario, Canada, where the practice of comparable worth is more common, day-care centers are actually closing down because parents can't afford to pay for the higher salaries, says Furchgott-Roth. But these charges turn out to be only partially true. Child-care centers in Ontario were threatened when a Progressive Conservative government succeeded the liberal New Democrats and slashed funding. But the centers have not closed down. After a court challenge and an enormous public outcry, the provincial government is still subsidizing pay equity for child-care workers (who, even with subsidies, earn an average of only $16,000 a year).

State employment officials in Minnesota and Wisconsin, two states with comparable-worth laws, say that any labor shortages have far more to do with the tight labor market than with comparable worth. "There's a lot of flexibility in the law," says Faith Zwemke, Minnesota's pay-equity coordinator. "For information technology people, for instance, we can give them signing bonuses and let them advance faster within the parameters of the policy."

Some male workers inevitably do resent women getting increases. "But many men can see pay equity as a family issue," says Karen Nussbaum of the AFL-CIO. A recent poll by Democratic pollster Celinda Lake showed that six out of ten voters, both men and women, said equal pay was good for families.

Pay-equity advocates had better be patient and persistent. The market has been biased against women at least since it was written in the Old Testament that when a vow offering is made to God, it should be based on the value of the person, and "[if] a male, from the age of twenty years up to the age of sixty years, your assessment shall be fifty silver shekels . . . and if it is a female, your assessment shall be thirty shekels." At this rate, winning equal pay may take a long time.

Two Cheers for the Earned Income Tax Credit

It's Great, but No Substitute for Decent Wages

JARED BERNSTEIN

I like the Earned Income Tax Credit (EITC) a lot. I also really like brownies with gobs of vanilla ice cream and hot fudge. But I don't have them for breakfast, lunch, and dinner.

The EITC—a refundable tax credit that subsidizes the wages of low-income workers—is everyone's darling. New Democrats love it. President Clinton expanded it significantly in his first budget and in 2000 proposed another expansion. Almost every economist willing to use tax policy to help low-income families supports it. Even the right is on board. When congressional Republicans wanted to delay EITC payments to help make their budget numbers add up, candidate George W. Bush (still in compassionate mode) went after them with vigor for trying to balance the budget "on the backs of the poor." And in recent testimony around a proposed minimum-wage increase, House Republicans were falling all over each other to heap praise on the EITC as a far better alternative (though none was proposing to increase it).

But is it possible, as with brownies and ice cream, to have too much of this good thing? Are there unintended effects of the EITC that might be worth considering?

The EITC is clearly raising the living standards of low-income working families. Furthermore, the fact that it is tied to work has largely insulated it from partisan attack and has even allowed for its expansion in this era when social-welfare spending is so highly scrutinized. Yet the EITC is not perfect. Some of its benefits surely end up subsidizing employers, who would likely have to raise their wage offers in the absence of the program. More important (since this wage effect is probably small), relying solely on tax policy to raise the incomes of low-wage workers is a serious mistake. We also need policies that focus directly on raising pretax wages. Otherwise, we face the likelihood of a perpetually expanding low-end labor market, with jobs that fail to pay a living wage and thus require ever-increasing taxpayer subsidy.

The EITC dates to 1975. The original idea was to offset the bite of payroll taxes on low-wage workers in low-income families. Since then, the credit has been expanded considerably. There are now three different schedules: a small credit for single-person households and childless couples, a much larger credit for families with one child, and a still larger credit for families with two or more children. And since eligibility is keyed to family income, the subsidy is quite finely targeted (rich kids with after-school jobs need not apply). As family income rises, EITC benefits initially grow, then level off, and then begin to phase out. A working parent with two children gets 40 cents in tax credit for each dollar earned up to an income level of $9,720. (These figures are for the year 2000.) The maximum annual benefit is thus $3,888. Then, starting at $12,690 in annual income for this type of family, the tax credit declines by 21 cents for each dollar earned, phasing out altogether at an annual income of $31,152. For a family with one child, the peak benefit is $2,353, and for a single person it's $353.

The key to the program is that the tax credit is refundable. Low-income families (those in the bottom 20 percent or so of the income distribution) owe no federal income tax and thus have no liability against which to deduct a tax benefit. But since the EITC is refundable, these workers receive a check from the IRS.

In 1997 the IRS paid out $30.6 billion in EITC claims to about 18.5 million persons. That's up from $6.6 billion in 1989 and $1.3 billion in 1975 (in nominal dollars). And we've gotten a lot for the money. As the Center on Budget and Policy Priorities has shown, in 1998 the EITC was responsible for lifting nearly 5 million persons out of poverty. A memo circulated by the Council of Economic Advisers at the time of the last minimum-wage increase made the important point that by itself the minimum wage would not lift a full-time working parent with two kids above the poverty line, but it would with the EITC. Moreover, as a wage subsidy, the EITC has avoided the political fate of welfare benefits. Progressives encounter little resistance when they argue that if Congress wants people to work, it needs to make work pay.

But there are two questions worth asking about this laudable program. First, is it possible that the EITC is subsidizing employers as opposed to low-wage workers? Second, does it make sense to depend so thoroughly on the tax system to "make work pay"?

Tax subsidies invariably leak. They almost always subsidize, at least in part, something that would have happened anyway, and they thus create a windfall for whoever would have paid for it. The structure of the EITC probably mitigates this problem considerably, but there are certainly some employers of low-wage workers who would have offered a higher wage in the absence of the tax credit.

Imagine a tight labor market where workers will not accept a job that produces take-home pay lower than, say, $300 per week. If employers know that the taxpayer will make up the difference through the EITC, then they can get away with a lower wage offer. Thus, the EITC partially transfers income from taxpayers to employers, whose labor costs for low-wage workers are artificially suppressed by the tax credit. The transfer can only be partial because the credit has to leave the worker better off. Otherwise, she has no incentive to participate.

No one has figured out the extent to which this income transfer is occurring, but tax and labor economists generally agree that the credit is partially subsidizing employers—and that the effect is probably small. One reason is the design of the tax credit. Employers do not necessarily know who's covered by the EITC, since nearly everyone elects to take it in a lump sum from the IRS, not as a paycheck benefit. Nor do employers know a job applicant's income or family structure, both of which determine the amount of the credit. So it is hard for employers to gauge how low a wage they can offer.

Still, by inducing an increase in the supply of low-wage labor, the EITC probably lowers market wage offers slightly across the board. When work is more financially attractive, more people want to work, which can lead to lower wages. And the EITC, in tandem with welfare reform, has significantly increased the supply of low-wage labor. Since 1989 the employment rate of single mothers has increased from 58 percent to 71 percent. (There is some evidence of reduced employment among those on the down slope of the subsidy schedule, where the subsidy falls as earnings rise. But on a net basis, the credit has been found to raise labor supply—as, indeed, it was meant to do—especially among the lowest-wage workers.)

These supply effects have been more than offset, however, during the recent highly touted economic recovery, by a much more important determinant of wages: a low unemployment rate. In fact, low wages did not budge until two things happened, both circa 1996: The minimum wage was raised, and the unemployment rate began its downward trek from 5.7 percent in January 1996 to 4 percent four years later. In the earlier years of the recovery, between 1989 and 1996, the real pretax wage at the twentieth percentile fell 2.4 percent; since 1996 it has risen 8.1 percent. But these wage gains should not be taken to mean that increased labor supply—stemming from the expanded EITC, welfare reform, and the higher minimum wage—hasn't had an impact on the low-wage sector and won't in the future. It's just that the demand for low-wage workers has recently grown even faster.

More troubling are the effects of relying on the EITC—as many progressives and all New Democrats do—as our sole near-term wage policy. To be sure, it is largely due to the increase in the EITC in the first Clinton budget that the federal tax system has become more progressive. (Taxes also rose for those at the very top.) According to Congressional Budget Office tabulations, between 1989 and 1999, the average income of the bottom 40 percent of households fell by 3 percent on a pretax basis, but was unchanged in the post-tax distribution. Most of this difference is due to the EITC, which has helped not only to offset the regressive payroll tax, as originally intended, but also to make up for some of the earnings decline experienced by these families.

So what's wrong with that? Well, for one thing, we cannot depend on the tax system—or, more precisely, on the taxpayers—to keep repairing the damage caused by market outcomes. Except for the past few years, when tight job markets and the minimum-wage increase did begin to lift the earnings of the lowest-paid workers, pretax wages have been falling for two decades. Even with the recent gains, the twentieth-percentile male wage, adjusted for inflation, is still 13 percent below its 1979 level. Low-wage women workers have not done as badly: Their twentieth-percentile wage in 1999 was only 1 percent below where it was in 1979, but their tenth-percentile wage, which is more closely tied to the minimum wage, was 9 percent lower.

These negative trends in pretax wages have nothing to do with the tax system. As my colleague Larry Mishel likes to say, "It's not what the government's been taking out. It's what employers have failed to put in." It is market forces that have led to persistent increases in wage and income inequality since the late 1970s, and while progressive tax shifts (like the EITC expansion) have helped to slow the process, this approach cannot go on indefinitely. Even if conservative politicians would agree to such an agenda, it would be bad economic policy.

No matter how much we like the EITC, progressives mustn't punt on the pretax distribution, leaving it to the tax system to clean up the mess. The tax credit should be seen as part of a package that involves both pretax and post-tax interventions in the low-wage labor market.

The low-wage labor market is very much a part of the American economic landscape. Various silly reports that try to argue that the new jobs of the past decades are mostly good jobs are patently false (though it's equally false to argue that all the new jobs are for hamburger flippers). We have a booming low-wage sector, driven by both the increase in demand for low-wage services and the fact that these jobs are relatively cheap to create. In *The State of Working America*, which I co-authored with Larry Mishel and John Schmitt, we show that the share of the workforce earning low wages has actually expanded slightly since the late 1970s, growing from 24 percent in 1979 to 26 percent in 1998. (We define a low wage as any wage up to the amount needed to lift a family of four to the poverty line with full-year work, which was $8.26 an hour in 1999.) In fact, among the ten occupations that the Bureau of Labor Statistics predicts will add the most jobs over the next ten years, five are low-wage positions, including retail salespersons, cashiers, and home health aides.

Whether this strikes you as a good or bad thing depends on your perspective. For a welfare reformer or for someone who believes that all you need is a start, an expanding low-wage sector is a blessing. For someone who appreciates the generally low mobility in low-wage jobs—how infrequently they are stepping-stones to better jobs—the blessing is much more mixed. However, in either case, what's clear is that most low-wage workers are not likely to earn enough to meet their basic needs for safe housing, food, reliable child care, health insurance, and transportation. That is why the vast majority of analysts who examine the economic opportunities facing low-income working families advocate the use of subsidies such as the EITC. But what led us to a situation where we have such a large low-wage labor market in need of such extensive subsidies?

You might think to blame a decline in the skill level of low-wage workers. But, in fact, as Heidi Hartmann and I show in a recent paper, the average level of education in the low-wage labor market is considerably higher now than in earlier periods. We only go back to 1979 in our work, but we show that the share of workers in the low-wage sector with at least some college education has risen by 13.5 percent since then. This is, of course, simply the outcome of long-term educational upgrading of the labor market. But so what? The fact is that we now have a more skilled (at least in terms of years of education) yet lower-paid low-wage worker.

A number of factors have contributed: the well-known shift from manufacturing to services, hastened by years of trade imbalances in manufactured goods; the related decline in unions and their slow (though accelerating) inroads into low-paying sectors; the long-term decline in the real value of the minimum wage, which, even with recent increases, remains 27 percent below its late 1960s peak; the inflow of large numbers of low-skilled immigrants; the fact that throughout the 1980s and early 1990s the monetary authorities mistakenly believed that the noninflationary unemployment rate (the so-called NAIRU) was 6 to 6.5 percent (a mistake that led to a looser labor market than was necessary and thus made low-wage jobs cheaper).

And the increase in economic inequality has reinforced these changes. In our economy, people want more and more cheap services. Those of us who work many hours want dry cleaning, takeout, videos, child care (which has no business being a low-wage job), and twenty-four-hour markets. And as long as low-wage labor is cheap and plentiful, we'll probably keep getting them.

On the other hand, let me tell you about my shoelaces. If you run into me and I'm wearing my black shoes (I also have brown ones— the full D.C. footwear complement), take a look at my shoelaces. You will notice that the right one is a shorter version of the left, threaded through every other hole. The reason is that while I was at a recent conference in Germany, my shoelace broke. Each day, as the conference wound down around 5:00 p.m., I went out to buy new shoelaces. And each day I confronted a bunch of closed shops. For the lack of low-end services available after work, I had the very un-American experience of not being able to buy what I wanted when I wanted it.

There simply isn't a comparable low-wage service sector in much of Europe because higher wages (both pretax and post-tax), more union coverage, and more social protections mean it costs much more to create a low-wage job there. Europeans also have regulations about when shops must close. (And they have more unemployment and less job growth, about which more in a moment.) But the point is, we have set up our economy in such a way as to encourage the creation of millions of low-wage jobs. The signs here point to the low road. The Europeans tend to block that route.

If we made low-wage jobs more expensive, we might create fewer jobs, but they would be of higher quality. If the American minimum wage were significantly increased, and then indexed to prices or productivity, it could have this effect. Our current minimum wage does not because it remains at a level that neither discourages low-wage job formation nor provides low-wage workers with enough income to meet their basic needs, and also because its value begins to erode the minute it's introduced. Back in 1968, full-time work at the minimum wage put a worker with two children about $1,300 (in 1999 dollars) above the poverty line. Today, she would be $2,700 below the line. Of course, once you add in the EITC—which didn't exist in the late 1960s—her family's income once again surpasses the poverty line, in this case by a few hundred dollars. Over the past three decades, the cost of maintaining an antipoverty wage has been shifted from employers to taxpayers.

Increasing union power in the low-wage sector would also raise low wages, and recent rumblings suggest this sector is ripe for organizing (see Harold Meyerson, "A Clean Sweep"), while the labor movement has made it clear that it will be making an effort to organize low-wage immigrants.

Mandating employer-provided health care is another idea along the same route. And, of course, the education and training of our low-wage workforce is a key to raising wages. I deemphasize this not because

I think it's less important than the other ideas noted above, but because it already has a plethora of defenders.

But does this path not guarantee the high rates of unemployment and low rates of job growth facing Europe? In fact, no. The case that Europe's labor-market problems stem from its labor-market protections is a very weak one. Numerous studies, including work by the ideologically middle-of-the-road Organisation of Economic Co-operation and Development, show that the pattern of unemployment in Europe is inconsistent with this hypothesis, while other studies show that macroeconomic factors, such as unnecessarily tight monetary policy, go much further in explaining the differences between our labor market outcomes and theirs.

This is not to say that raising the cost of low-wage jobs would have no effect on job creation. While I guarantee you that the low-wage job market is a far cry from the competitive job market we learned about in grad school, it's still the case that significantly increasing the pretax wage does engender the possibility of less low-wage job creation. But it just as certainly engenders the possibility of creating better jobs. We cannot and should not regulate our labor market to the extent of some European economies, but by raising pretax wages, we could go some way toward blocking the low road.

We have a low-wage labor market problem in this country, and the EITC is an essential part of the solution. But it cannot be the sole solution. Unless we rely on other strategies for improving pretax earnings in the low-wage sector, the living standards of low-income families will be largely dependent on the tax system. And when the current tight market for low-wage labor unwinds and real wages start to head south, we will be stuck trying to ratchet up the EITC year after year. That can only work for so long.

Welfare That Works

The Case for More Generous Formulas to Reward Paid Work

GORDON L. BERLIN

Through recent decades, America's social welfare policies have oscillated between two contradictory impulses. The 1960s were marked by a campaign against poverty; in the 1980s, welfare policy was increasingly concerned with fighting dependency. By the early 1990s, when welfare rolls hit an all-time high, the fear of unintended consequences—that welfare was discouraging work and marriage, and encouraging out-of-wedlock childbearing—led to reforms that limited how long someone could receive welfare benefits, the incorporation of strict work requirements, and, thus, the end of welfare as we knew it.

At issue is an age-old conundrum: The jobless poor need cash benefits to escape destitution and to have any hope of moving up. Yet cash benefits can reduce the incentive to work (and, some believe, to marry)—especially if policies make the welfare package more attractive than a low-wage job (or a low-wage husband). Under the old welfare system, many families ended up no better off financially for having gone to work. Beyond losing cash benefits, families that suddenly moved from welfare to work incurred new expenses, such as transportation and child care, and also risked losing government health-care benefits.

Would it be possible to design a system of cash support that encouraged work, reduced poverty, and improved the well-being of families and children without deepening welfare dependency? A system in which recipients could retain both necessary in-kind services such as child care and cash subsidies for an extended period as they became experienced workers?

The Manpower Demonstration Research Corporation (MDRC), a nonprofit group that conducts demonstration programs and evaluations, has worked with federal, state, and local policy makers to launch three large-scale experiments aimed at determining what difference work incentives packaged together with other changes (including elimination of various disincentives to work and marry) would make in rewarding work, minimizing dependency, and lifting workers and their families out of poverty. The experiments began prior to the 1996 welfare-reform legislation mandating time limits on welfare, but the three-year follow-up findings from two of the experiments shine new light on the triple challenge of increasing work and reducing both dependency and poverty in this era of time-limited welfare.

Three Experiments

Acting independently of one another, policy makers in Minnesota, Wisconsin, and Canada set out to design and test alternatives to the traditional safety-net system: Rather than paying people when they did not work, these alternatives aimed to support people when they did. The evidence from ongoing rigorous evaluations of these programs conducted by MDRC is encouraging: When cash supplements were paid on top of earnings, particularly to long-term welfare recipients, these programs increased employment and income, lowered the fraction of families with below-poverty-level incomes, reduced the incidence of divorce, and generally improved family and child well-being.

The results have important implications. More than forty states now attempt to bolster low-wage workers by disregarding some earnings when calculating welfare benefits. Pennsylvania disregards 50 percent of all earnings, while California disregards the first $225 plus 50 percent of remaining earnings. In effect, this liberalization of "earned-income disregards" allows welfare recipients to work and receive cash payments that supplement their earnings from entry-level jobs. These little-noticed "make work pay" provisions were part of the time-limited welfare changes states made in reaction to the 1996 federal welfare reforms—suggesting that states were as concerned about poverty reduction as they were about dependency reduction. States also made changes designed to keep families together, namely elimination of the rule requiring two-parent families to lose welfare eligibility as soon as one parent works more than 100 hours a month, regardless of earnings.

While the founding impetus was different for each of the make-work-pay programs MDRC studied—the Minnesota approach was launched by state government; in Milwaukee, Wisconsin, a coalition of community groups set up a targeted program for specific areas of the city; and in Canada, two provinces worked in partnership with the national government—these three shared an underlying approach: They attempted to make low-wage work pay by providing work incentives in the form of monthly cash payments. These payments were made only when people worked, and the amount of each month's cash payment depended on that month's earnings.

These were not work-for-your-benefits "workfare" models. Rather, the idea was to create real, monetary incentives—to increase the payoff of low-wage work through work-conditioned earnings supplements. All three programs encouraged welfare recipients to work full time (at least thirty hours a week), either by tying incentive payments to full-time work or by requiring those who were not working full time to participate in job preparation services. Aggressive outreach and communication about the value of the incentives were hallmarks of these programs. In each place, of course, the welfare safety-net system continued to operate. In Canada and Milwaukee, where the programs operated outside of the welfare system, people who lost their jobs (and thus their work incentive payments) could return to welfare by reapplying. In Minnesota, those who lost their jobs were automatically converted back to the traditional welfare benefit structure, without applying.

Here's a closer look:

The Minnesota Family Investment Program (MFIP) used the welfare system (which combined food stamps and welfare into one cash grant) to reward work by changing the way earned income was treated: It increased both the "earned-income disregard" and the basic benefit level for workers. These changes had the effect of increasing a worker's income by as much as $250 a month above what the basic welfare system would have paid someone taking a job. In addition, for long-term welfare recipients who were not working at least thirty hours a week, MFIP required participation in employment-focused services designed to help them find jobs. Failure to participate could result in a 10 percent grant reduction. For two-parent families, the program also eliminated the 100-hour rule. MFIP first operated as a pilot program; in modified form, it became Minnesota's statewide welfare program in 1998.

A family assigned to MFIP would meet with an eligibility specialist to understand how benefits would be affected when work began. Caseworkers enthusiastically conveyed the "work pays" message; for the first time, they could honestly tell recipients they would clearly be better off if they went to work. Long-term welfare recipients (two years or more) who were working less than thirty hours a week were then referred to an MFIP-contracted service provider and a case manager who would regularly reinforce the "work pays" message and help to develop an employment plan that could include education and training. For two-parent families, the participation requirement kicked in after six months. When a parent got a job, MFIP would help arrange and pay for child care, continue her Medicaid benefits, and establish a new benefit structure to supplement her earnings.

The Canadian Self-Sufficiency Project (SSP) tested a work-based alternative to welfare. It paid a substantial monthly earnings supplement for up to three years to long-term, single-parent welfare recipients who left welfare and worked full time (at least thirty hours a week)—as much as $400 a month above the amount they would have received if they had worked and remained on welfare. SSP, which ran from 1992 through 1999, operated outside the welfare system; it was administered by private agencies in Vancouver, British Columbia, and parts of New Brunswick. Participation was voluntary.

Single parents who had been on welfare for a year or more were contacted by a private social services agency and invited to a three-hour workshop, where worksheets and exercises were used to explain how SSP would affect their income if they found full-time jobs and left welfare. The typical recipient who received about $10,000 a year on welfare was shown that if she took a job for thirty hours a week or more, her earnings plus her SSP supplement would total about $20,000, assuming she worked full time for the entire year. Once working, each month she would complete a voucher, attach her pay stub, and submit it to the SSP office; staff there would verify that total hours met the thirty-hour-a-week eligibility threshold, and then calculate her supplement payment and deposit it in her bank account.

Milwaukee's New Hope Project was a community antipoverty initiative designed to test a comprehensive set of financial and other supports for low-income workers. It was open to all low-income people living in two target areas and offered a package of incentives consisting of earnings supplements plus child-care and health-care subsidies and—for people who could not find jobs—access to temporary community-service jobs. Participants had to work at least thirty hours a week to receive New Hope's incentives package, and they could be eligible for up to three years. The program operated from 1994 through 1998.

New Hope staff flooded the neighborhood with flyers and went door to door, reaching out to working and nonworking residents. Individuals who enrolled and were employed full time were asked for documentation of hours worked and wages. They were interviewed about their child-care and health-insurance needs, after which staff calculated benefit payments, signed each recipient up with one of the program's health-care providers, helped arrange child care (if the person had children), and made payments to the chosen provider. People who were not working full time were helped to find a job. Those who could not find one were offered a temporary community-service job. No one who worked less than thirty hours a week was able to receive benefits, but, because of the community jobs, no one was denied the opportunity to do so.

The studies were unusually rigorous. A random, lottery-like process was used to assign welfare recipients in MFIP and SSP, or, in New Hope's case, a broad cross section of low-income people, either to a group that was eligible for the program's work-incentive payments (e.g., the MFIP group) or to a group that was not (a control group eligible for the regular welfare program). The effect or "impact" of the program was measured according to differences in employment and other outcomes between the two groups.

By conditioning incentive payments on full-time work, the programs increased both work and income among single parents at risk of long-term welfare dependency, without incurring many of the unintended negative consequences on employment among the working poor that have plagued past policies. The employment and earnings gains among long-term welfare recipients were among the largest found in any previously evaluated welfare-to-work programs; the income gains and accompanying poverty reductions were unprecedented. These economic gains were the catalyst for a chain of mostly positive, and in some cases extraordinary, effects on families and children. More employable groups—welfare applicants, two-parent families, and groups that were working full time when they first learned about the programs—also benefited, but not as consistently. Overall costs rose, however, as the amount paid out in earnings supplements exceeded the welfare savings that resulted when more people went to work.

Smart Money

When work-incentive programs were linked to participation mandates or were conditioned on full-time work, they substantially increased the employment, earnings, and total income of long-term welfare recipients. By the second and third year of follow-up, the Minnesota and Canada programs increased annual employment rates relative to a control group that was not eligible for work-incentive payments by a fourth to a third, earnings by one- to two-fifths, and before-tax income by a sixth to a fourth. For example, over a period of nearly three years, MFIP increased quarterly employment rates by 35 percent (50 percent for MFIP versus 37 percent for the control group), while quarterly earnings were 23 percent higher ($955 for MFIP versus $779 for the control group).

Not surprisingly, given the rules governing each program, most of the effects of the three program were on full-time employment, with cascading effects on job retention and advancement. At its peak, the SSP program nearly doubled the full-time employment rate (29 percent for MFIP versus 16 percent for the control group). Job-retention rates were high—two of every three people who got a job because of MFIP or SSP stayed employed for at least a year. There was evidence of wage growth in both programs as well: In SSP, about half of those employed experienced wage growth of more than 10 percent over two years. Full-time employment was key to both job retention and wage advancement.

Moreover, the increased income that long-term welfare recipients obtained typically led to a substantial decline in both poverty and the poverty gap—that is, roughly an 11 percent drop in the number of people with incomes below the poverty line, as well as a sizable decrease in the size of the average gap between a recipient's income and the poverty line.

The evidence also showed that participants spent as much as half of their increased income on basic necessities—food, clothing, housing, and child care—a sign of previous impoverishment. Moreover, people made an effort to increase their assets by opening savings accounts and taking other actions; in SSP, the fraction of people with $500 or more in savings rose by nearly 30 percent.

Like the Earned Income Tax Credit (EITC) and other policies that redistribute income, these work-incentive programs typically increased receipt of transfer payments, resulting in modest increases in transfer payment amounts (6 to 14 percent higher than the welfare payments made to a control group). At the same time, the share of people relying solely on welfare declined substantially as more people combined work and earnings supplements.

These extra costs bought remarkable changes in family life and child outcomes. Incidents of domestic violence decreased 18 percent in MFIP (49 percent for MFIP versus 60 percent for the control group), while marriage rates increased (11 percent of the MFIP group was married three years later versus 7 percent of the control group). In SSP, marriage increased by a like amount in New Brunswick—a heavily Catholic province—but decreased in British Columbia, suggesting that cultural norms also influence whether work and income gains will encourage "independence" or marriage.

The data suggested improvements in several child outcomes as well, particularly for children ages two to nine when the programs began, including better performance in school, higher test scores, and fewer behavioral problems. For adolescents there was some suggestion of negative effects. With less parental supervision, adolescents may have been more likely to engage in minor delinquency behavior and experiment with alcohol, smoking, and possibly drugs.

For welfare applicants, the incentives-only program model in Minnesota, without participation requirements or full-time work conditions, had more limited effects, modestly increasing employment and income but not earnings. The New Hope program did increase employment, earnings, and income for people who were not working full time when they learned about that program, although the effects were smaller than with MFIP or SSP.

Among two-parent recipient families, MFIP was responsible for a dramatic increase in marriage, primarily because of a reduction in divorce and separation: At the end of the third year of follow-up, 67 percent of MFIP two-parent families were still married, compared with 48.5 percent of Aid to Families with Dependent Children (AFDC) recipients—a 38.1 percent increase. The program did not affect the likelihood that at least one parent would work, although the second earner in two-parent families typically cut back, suggesting that MFIP's effort to make work pay relieved stress on two-parent families. Total income still rose because supplement payment amounts exceeded the earnings decline; this extra income, coupled with a higher likelihood of staying married, led to a substantial increase in home ownership among the MFIP group (37 percent versus 18 percent).

Among the other findings:

- Program designs that conditioned incentives on full-time work or coupled them with a participation obligation, when also combined with employment services, appear to have produced the largest impacts.
- In contrast to findings on traditional welfare programs, which re-

duced benefits when people worked, there was little evidence of unintended reductions in work effort among the working poor. They may have reduced the number of hours worked (often by cutting down on overtime, as in New Hope), but employment rates did not decline. Nor was there evidence of large "entry effects," whereby the working poor quit their jobs to enter the welfare rolls and gain access to these highly targeted programs (these effects were experimentally tested in SSP).

- There were positive impacts on earnings, on top of any gains that might have resulted from the federal EITC program (which uses the tax system to pay cash supplements to low-income workers). This suggests that work-incentive programs, particularly those targeted at welfare recipients, can be an effective means of further increasing income and reducing poverty among single parents.

- For long-term welfare recipients, a dollar spent on work incentives yielded more than a dollar in increased income. For example, in SSP, every extra dollar the government paid in work incentives produced another dollar in earnings gains, for a total after-tax income gain of more than $2. The programs were not as efficient for two-parent families or the working poor; a dollar in benefits yielded less than a dollar in income.

- Financial incentives, work requirements, and services each made distinct contributions to the programs' effects. In MFIP, incentives were critical for increasing income and reducing poverty, and produced many of the effects on family and child well-being, whereas the participation mandate drove the full-time work and earnings and reduced reliance on welfare effects. In SSP, the incentive accounted for nearly all of the program's effects on work, income, and children. New Hope's employment effects were driven by the incentives package and the community-service jobs, while the health and child-care effects accounted for reductions in stress.

The programs were not a panacea. In Canada, only about a third of those eligible for the program ever took advantage of its earnings supplements, although that number rose to 50 percent when incentives were combined with job-search services. By comparison, in Minnesota, where both full- and part-time work were supplemented, about three-quarters of those eligible took advantage of the program.

Political Values

The findings pose two philosophical issues: What constitutes dependency, and how to choose between universal and targeted strategies for reducing poverty? On the dependency question, there is consistent evidence across the three studies that earnings supplements increase work and reduce poverty, but, by one measure, dependency arguably rises, albeit modestly. For example, in MFIP, 85 percent of the group received benefits (welfare when they did not work, earnings supplements when they did), while 81 percent of the control group did. Conversely, by another measure, dependency falls quite substantially—54 percent of the control group relied solely on welfare, while only 42 percent of the MFIP group did. The two effects are inevitable: Incentives programs reward some people who would have gone to work anyway, while they provide incentives to people who would not have worked otherwise. In these programs, the latter effect is clearly larger than the former. And, don't forget, increased benefits for the former group meant more income, less poverty, and improved child and family outcomes without a significant decrease in employment rates.

On the question of universal versus targeted programs, there is evidence to support either position in these findings. In favor of targeting—as one moves up the employability ladder to more employable welfare applicants, then to two-parent families, then to working-poor families—effects on employment, earnings, and income begin to decline, in part because there is not much room to affect employment in populations that work a lot already. But there are offsetting gains in favor of more universal approaches to consider as well. As Frank Levy explains in *The New Dollars and Dreams,* low-income two-parent families adjusted to twenty-three years of stagnant real earnings (1973–96) by sending both parents into the workplace, a strategy that created new stresses on families and children. Hours reductions by the second earner in MFIP two-parent families and among the full-time employed group in New Hope appear to have relieved some of this pressure, resulting in less family splitting (MFIP), less stress, and better outcomes for children (New Hope).

Policy Implications

In practical terms, the choice between universal and targeted strategies for making work pay is a choice between expanding the universal EITC program, which uses the tax system to supplement the pay of low-wage workers, and making changes to federal and/or state welfare programs operating under the Temporary Assistance for Needy Families (TANF) block grant created by the 1996 federal welfare reform bill. Increasing the generosity of the EITC avoids welfare's stigma, inequity, and bureaucracy, but there are disadvantages: The cost would be enormous, there is a risk of additional work reductions among working-class households as the credit moves further up the income stream, and, because the credit comes at the end of the year and is not well understood, it might not have the same work-inducing effects among more disadvantaged populations as a targeted program.

Using the TANF welfare system to make work pay produces a mirror image of pro and con arguments: On the one hand, the gains per person will be larger, the costs lower, and marketing easier; yet, on the other hand, the welfare system as currently structured is not well suited to supporting the working poor, and, most concerning of all, welfare caseloads have fallen by half since 1994, so recent welfare leavers would not benefit. Perhaps the most convincing arguments in favor of using the TANF structure are these: (1) MFIP and New Hope's effects occurred on top of the EITC; (2) most state welfare laws already include make-work-pay provisions; (3) TANF is a funding source, not a program, and thus is flexible enough to address at least some of the mentioned shortcomings, including being used to support a supplemental state EITC program.

Indeed, as welfare rolls have decreased, states have accumulated a large and growing surplus of federal dollars—$7 billion or higher by most estimates. If states do not spend these resources, the budget pressures created by the so-called "pay as you go" provisions now required in each year's budget bill may mean that Congress will reduce the federal contribution to the welfare block grant, effectively eliminating the surplus in future appropriations.

A Contradiction

But first, a basic contradiction must be resolved. States have put time limits on the total number of months families can receive welfare benefits (typically sixty months, sometimes fewer), which strongly discourage continued receipt of welfare assistance. As a result, when welfare recipients take jobs, the welfare system's more generous disregard policies have the perverse effect of holding job-takers on the welfare rolls, where they receive reduced grants and continue using up their lifetime limit of federal (and, in some cases, state) welfare benefits. This, in effect, perpetuates welfare's age-old conflict between reducing poverty and reducing dependency.

Moreover, why use work incentives to make work pay when time limits will have the same effect while also reducing costs? The answer depends on the importance policy makers place on reducing poverty among single-parent families with children. Limiting welfare will raise employment rates, but given the labor market's new insistence on skills, welfare recipients are most likely to get low-wage jobs with little prospect of earnings growth. Disposable income, even after receipt of the EITC, will likely remain well below the poverty line.

What are the implications for states that want to reduce poverty and dependency (defined as those relying solely on welfare) while encouraging work? First, states should consider separating time-limited welfare from work-incentive initiatives by stopping the clock on recipients' welfare time limits when they work full time (thirty hours a week or more). Then, when recipients do get jobs, they can leave time-limited welfare and join a newly created program for the working poor. This program could offer a range of supports, from work incentives to child care, health care, and information on the EITC. Illinois now stops the clock for anyone working more than twenty-five hours a week. Both Canada's SSP and Milwaukee's New Hope made their incentive payments only when someone worked at least thirty hours a week, and both programs were run outside the welfare system. New Hope's hours rule limited the work reductions among full-time workers to cutbacks in overtime work, and SSP's rule encouraged people who would not have worked at all to work full time—an important element in any long-term effort to attain self-sufficiency.

Second, states might make the incentive for full-time work more generous. When researchers simulated the effect of running an SSP-type program instead of the more modest disregards states have used in the past, the results suggested that an SSP-type program would have produced large increases in the number of long-term welfare recipients working full time and large increases in income, at only a modest net increase in costs. The magnitude of the simulated gains indicates that they would likely exceed those achieved by the states' current versions of enhanced earnings disregards.

Third, a more generous incentive payment could be structured to encourage and reward asset accumulation. Incentive payments could be broken into two components—one to supplement earnings and another to supplement savings. For example, if participants managed to save $1,500 of the $5,000 or more, their incomes could increase annually; if incentive funds matched those savings, over the course of three to five years, many participants might be able to afford to buy a home.

Fourth, if the stigma and inequity that accompany a targeted program are judged too high a price to pay despite its efficiency, policy makers might consider establishing a supplemental state EITC program or increasing the generosity of the federal universal EITC program, but only for people who work at least thirty hours a week. This strategy would encourage full-time employment and limit the work-hour reductions among full-time workers while retaining the part-time work benefits of the existing EITC program for single parents, whose parenting responsibilities may preclude full-time work. Policy makers might also consider an even more generous EITC program for married parents, to promote work and marriage.

The mounting TANF surplus indicates that states can afford to help make work pay. Indeed, most state welfare reforms have intended to do just that. Presumably, if supporting people when they do not work does not comport with America's values, then supporting people when they do work would. While additional experimentation is warranted, particularly to confirm the marriage effects of incentive programs, the evidence amassed so far on the economic effects of making work pay is compelling. The benefits are substantial, the costs can be modest, and the risks appear to be minimal.

Skills and the Wage Collapse

Better Education and Training Are Only Half the Story

DAVID HOWELL

Despite the record economic expansion and near full employment, wages for the bottom fifth of the workforce are still far below their 1979 levels. Well over one-fifth of the male workforce earns poverty-level wages (22.5 percent in 1997), a figure almost twice as high as in the early 1970s (12.8 percent in 1973). This wage collapse is a big part of the sharply rising inequality experienced by American workers over the past two decades.

The conventional explanation rests on the view that wages mainly reflect the interaction between the demand for and supply of skills. The collapse at the bottom, in this view, is simply a consequence of the failure of individuals to provide the skills employers require in an increasingly computerized global economy. The remedy follows directly: We need a more highly skilled workforce. This story is very plausible—and substantially wrong.

To be sure, more highly skilled workers do earn higher wages, other things being equal. But other very important things are not equal. While advanced technology in a globalized and deregulated economy has surely changed the skills sought by employers, there is little evidence that the rising demand for skills in the American workplace was any greater in the years after 1980 than in preceding decades, when the wages of low-skill workers were rising.

So what is different now? Beginning in the mid-1970s, public policy and management strategies have reflected a profound national ideological shift toward laissez-faire markets. At the same time, we have witnessed a revolution in information technologies, which has greatly facilitated communication and transportation. These two concurrent developments have made it far easier, and indeed necessary, to shop around for the most productive, lowest-wage workers in the world. Globalization, with its dislocations, has also brought to our shores millions of new, low-skilled immigrant workers willing to work for even lower wages.

The collapse in earnings is not mainly a skills problem caused by the demands of a new computerized economy. After all, there has been no wage collapse for the least skilled in other developed countries. Rather, the problem is declining worker bargaining power in increasingly global and deregulated labor markets.

Who the New Economy Hurt

Only those at the very top of the earnings distribution have seen real wage gains over the past two decades. Most have experienced declines. Median earners, adjusted for the costs of living, made $11.46 in 1979, $11.18 in 1989, and just $10.82 in 1997 (in 1997 dollars). Even those nearer the top of the earnings distribution, at the seventieth percentile, saw their earnings fall from $15.69 to $15.08. While the economy has grown, productivity has increased and the number of millionaires sky-rocketed. Even those near the top, at the eightieth percentile, only broke even over this eighteen-year period. Only since 1998 have median wages begun a very modest recovery.

Of course, it was precisely the workers who could least afford lower take-home pay who were hurt most by the "new economy." Those in the twentieth to fortieth deciles lost about 8 percent between 1979 and 1997; those in the tenth saw a collapse of 15 percent, from $6.42 to $5.46. These figures cover all workers. The picture looks far worse for male workers at all points in the wage distribution. Between the twenti-eth and fortieth deciles, male workers in 1997 earned about 18 percent less than they did in 1979. There has been a very slight reversal of these shifts since 1996, but it is too recent and too dependent on abnormally tight labor markets to be a reliable trend.

The earnings collapse has been concentrated among those with the least education and experience, particularly among men. For high school graduates with one to five years of work experience, earnings fell by a staggering 27 percent between 1979 and 1995. Even college gradu-ates with less than six years of work saw earnings decline by 11 percent. Except at the very top, only female college graduates with six or more years of experience have thrived in this booming economy, with earn-ings increasing by 21 percent. It's also true that American workers with less than a college degree are, by standard measures, far less skilled than most northern European workers. For example, among those aged six-teen to twenty-five, 55.5 percent in the United States placed "below an adequate threshold of literacy," defined as level 1 or 2 on the Interna-tional Adult Literacy Survey (IALS) tests in 1994–95. This contrasts with 44.4 percent in the United Kingdom, 34.2 percent in Germany, 23.6 percent in Belgium, 22.9 percent in the Netherlands, and 19.7 percent in Sweden.

Bad Timing

At first blush, this all seems quite consistent with the conventional wisdom. American workers indeed need higher skills. But the evidence does not point to technological shifts or skills deficits as the main *source* of the earnings problem. For starters, the timing is off. Most of the shift in the skill-intensity of employment (conventionally measured as the white-collar share of employment) between 1979 and the present occurred between 1980 and 1983, well before computers could have had large, economy-wide impacts.

Nor do wage trends seem to fit the story. The wage collapse took place between 1979 and 1994. The lowest-wage workers (tenth decile) fared the worst in the early 1980s, but their wages stabilized between 1984 and 1998, just when information technology began having a widespread impact in many workplaces. In contrast to the popular view that the lowest-skilled workers have experienced the greatest wage cuts, between 1984 and 1994 it was those in the middle of the distribution that fared the worst (in percentage terms). And if skill mismatch in the face of computerization is the main story, why the improvement since the mid-1990s? Are low-skill workers now much better matched to workplace technology than in the late 1980s, the end of the last boom? Hardly.

Moreover, many of the occupations that show large wage declines do not fit the conventional story. If computer-based technological change led to a massive demand shift against the least skilled, and this is the principal cause of the wage collapse, data on occupations and wages should reflect that. But the data present us with a much more complex and ambiguous picture. There turns out to be no statistical association between wage growth and employment growth across some 450 occupations in the 1984–97 period (or for either 1984–92 or 1989–97), and only a modest positive link between skill levels and wage growth.

In fact, some of our largest low-skill occupations have experienced very large wage declines (compared to the economy-wide average) at the same time that they've experienced large employment increases (relative to the economy-wide norm) over the 1984–97 period. These included cashiers, cooks, nurse's aides, orderlies and attendants, groundskeepers and gardeners, janitors, and truck drivers. Further confounding the conventional wisdom, all of these large, rapidly growing, declining-wage occupations showed increasing shares of workers with more than a high school degree, which is particularly striking given the large shares of immigrant workers in many of them. Indeed, five of these eight occupations showed increases in this measure of skill that were far above the average for all occupations.

Finally, the recent scholarly literature offers little evidence of particularly large or accelerating "skill-biased" demand shifts that could plausibly account for the unprecedented collapse of low-skill male wages since the 1970s. Nor have studies found a strong causal link between computerization and wages. (It turns out that pencil use has had about the same statistical effect on wages as computer use.)

So it is fair to ask: How did the technology/skills story become the conventional wisdom, and why has it persisted?

What Does Skill Have To Do With It?

The skills story is attractive intuitively: We are experiencing dramatic technological changes, and those with the highest educational credentials are unquestionably doing the best. But it is a simple supply-and-demand story that omits a lot of messy details about labor-market institutions, social norms, management strategies, and bargaining power.

Economists wedded to the usual story read the increase in overall earnings inequality in the 1980s and 1990s as just an increase in the "return to skill." Between the 1970s and 1990s, the share of college-educated workers increased dramatically, yet these workers saw huge gains relative to those with high school degrees or less. In a simple demand-and-supply world, a relative shift in the demand for highly skilled workers "must have" overwhelmed this increase in supply to produce the observed relative wage increases. Hence, the standard explanation for rising inequality.

There are two problems with this "must have" explanation. First, efforts by economists to actually measure demand and supply shifts by decade have produced no support for the requirement of this simple model that labor demand shifts in fact overwhelmed labor supply shifts in the 1980s, the decade in which most of the wage collapse occurred.

The second problem with the supply-demand logic is that other things matter. The minimum wage, union coverage, and the deregulation of a number of industries played key roles in the wage collapse. From a value of $6.29 in 1979 (1997 dollars), the minimum wage fell to $4.34 in 1989, a 31 percent decline. Although there were two increases between 1989 and 1991, by 1995 its value was only slightly higher, $4.48.

Two additional increases between 1995 and 1997 made a big difference, increasing the 1997 minimum wage to $5.15. Along with declining unemployment, these increases were probably a big part of the reason for the real-wage increase shown in the hourly wage figure between 1994 and 1998.

Another institutional shift has been the precipitous decline in union membership, from 24 percent of the workforce in 1979 to just 13.9 percent in 1998. Perhaps the best measure of union power, the number of days lost to strikes, also shows steady declines since the early 1970s. And concerning deregulation, we can take the example of truck drivers: Deregulation in the late 1970s facilitated a shift toward nonunion drivers. The result? Sharply falling average real wages for truck drivers between 1984 and 1997, a period of rising demand for drivers, sharply increasing educational attainment among drivers, and declining overall unemployment. Deregulation also undercut the pay of workers in industries as diverse as airlines, public utilities, and banks, all of which were once more intensely regulated than they are today. According to the best estimates in the economics literature, deregulation has cost workers up to $5.7 billion in trucking, $3.4 billion in airlines, and $5.1 billion in telecommunications.

It's About Bargaining Power

To understand the role of lost bargaining power in rising inequality, it pays to revisit the work of the early postwar labor relations specialists, such as Clark Kerr and John Dunlop, part of a long tradition of social scientists who look beyond the intersection of demand-and-supply schedules to account for real-world labor market outcomes. Work in

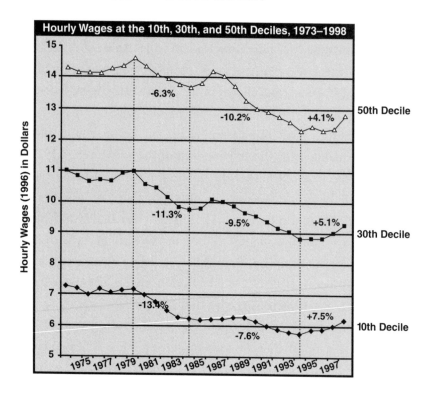

Hourly Wages at the 10th, 30th, and 50th Deciles, 1973–1998

this more "structural" tradition suggests that employers in fact offer a wide range of starting wages and wage increases for a given level of "skill," depending on the industry, the occupation, and the firm's management philosophy and competitive strategy.

Within a broad range set by demand-and-supply forces, by social norms, and by legal constraints, relative wages substantially reflect the outcomes of bargaining between workers and employers. In this view, several other institutional factors will all influence wage-setting and contribute to different wage outcomes for similarly skilled workers in similarly attractive jobs across establishments. These include imperfect information about worker performance, the importance of teamwork in production, the degree of market power in product markets, the share of labor in total costs, the collective power of workers, managerial preferences over competitive strategy, and government regulations.

With this institutional vision of the way wage-setting works, a very different story of the rising wage inequality emerges. It begins with the 1970s, a decade marked by declining productivity growth, rising unemployment, and inflation. On top of these difficulties, in the late 1970s workers and unions were faced with a marked ideological and institutional shift away from collective/public and toward competitive market solutions, much like earlier laissez-faire, antigovernment episodes in the 1920s and 1950s. Partly spurred by this ideological shift in the United States and in the United Kingdom, but also by rapid technological advances in communications and transportation and a growing role for Wall Street in corporate governance, the pace of globalization in production, trade, and financial movements accelerated, which in turn led to a rise in price competition.

In this new ideological and competitive context, labor markets were deregulated, trade barriers dismantled, the minimum wage allowed to decline sharply in real terms, and union power undermined. The available global supply of low-wage workers increased. These new conditions not only allowed, but required, firms to cut labor costs through the adoption of such strategies as wage concessions, the use of low-cost temporary labor and immigrant labor, and the relocation and/or outsourcing to low-labor-cost regions. Consequently, as economists Dani Rodrik and Adrian Wood have long argued, increasing trade and capital flows reduced U.S. worker bargaining power, especially for those least able to contest the wage cuts.

Indeed, legal immigration was allowed to reach its highest level since the first decades of the twentieth century, and current estimates put illegal immigration at six million. We have, in fact, made a political choice to pay large shares of immigrant workers poverty-level wages for their hard work. This is our official government policy, supported in particular by the self-interests of the farmers, small businesses, and upper-income families who rely on the services they provide.

The consequence of these changes in the effective (often poorly measured) supply of labor, in the deregulation of wage-setting, and in the social acceptability of paying the lowest wage possible is that changes in relative wages can be unrelated to changes in skill requirements. An alternative ideological, political, and institutional setting might have encouraged firms to take the "high road," in which costs are reduced not via wage and benefits cuts but through the use of more advanced technologies and more "employee-friendly" (and productivity-enhancing) governance structures and human-resource policies.

Can firms in the "new global economy" make choices to follow the high road? While not easily put to a statistical test, there is some supporting evidence. Based on his analysis of manufacturing plants of 3,000 firms with fewer than 500 employees, economist Dan Luria concludes that "clearly, in most industries, firms can now adopt recipes with very different mixes of wages, skill, technology, training, and basic management discipline." Luria's account suggests that the problem is, perhaps, less an acceleration of skill-biased technological change than political choices that have increased employer incentives to cut labor costs via wage cuts instead of through investment in advanced technologies. Economist Paul Osterman's *Securing Prosperity* provides a detailed map of a "high road" strategy.

But won't the higher wages that come with the labor market institutions and social policies that shelter workers from virulent wage competition simply produce higher unemployment? Harvard economist Larry Katz recently explained to a *New York Times* reporter that "[o]ne can say the Europeans have made a political decision that they are unwilling to tolerate as much income inequality as in the United States. But equity comes at the cost of job creation." And in his *Business Week* column, Gary Becker asserts that the employment problems of Europe are explained by "conventional interventions in labor markets that discourage companies from hiring workers." The obvious solution is "cutting taxes, subsidies, regulations, and controls over employment, wages, and new businesses."

Despite the pronouncements of leading liberal and conservative economists and the widespread acceptance in policy circles, the welfare-state-as-culprit story does a poor job of accounting for the rise in European unemployment. To be sure, unemployment has been a serious problem in much of Europe. But unemployment trends vary so widely across the Continent that it is almost impossible to generalize. Further, the distinctiveness of U.S. unemployment performance has been quite recent. It also turns out that standard measures of protective institutions and social policies are for the most part not closely correlated with unemployment levels or trends across Organisation for Economic Co-operation and Development nations. Unemployment rates are now falling in much of Europe, despite welfare states little changed from a decade ago, when the European unemployment crisis was at its peak.

And crucially, the skills dimension is missing. In the conventional story, the technology-driven shift in demand away from the least skilled is the shock that requires wage flexibility if unemployment is to be avoided. If this is so, the least skilled should be driving the upward movement of unemployment rates in Europe. But that has not been the case. Countries experiencing rapid increases in unemployment almost uniformly show rising rates across the skills distribution.

There is no question that in recent years the United States has been quite successful generating employment growth. But there is much more to the story than labor market flexibility. While the growing availability of a rising share of temporary, low wage, often immigrant workers has contributed to U.S. employment growth, as economists Alan Krueger and Jörn Steffan Pischke have argued, much of the U.S. employment advantage can be explained simply by much higher working-age population growth and greater product market flexibility in the United States. Until recently, the United States also had much more expansionary macroeconomic policies (via deficit spending), while key European economies were constrained by extremely restrictive monetary policies of the German Bundesbank. Further, the business cycle contributed to the rising gap: As the United States came out of a modest recession in the early 1990s, much of Europe went into one, magnifying the differential in unemployment rates. Most experts now recognize that Europe's famous labor market rigidity is not the leading culprit.

Beyond Wage Competition

In sum, America needs more well-trained workers, but the skill-mismatch story does not explain our massive growth in wage inequality. In a long-run (1940–90) perspective, there is little evidence of particularly large or accelerating skill-biased shifts in the demand for workers that could account for the unprecedented collapse of low and moderate-skill male wages since the late 1970s.

The skill-mismatch view leads either to a do-nothing strategy (leave it to the labor market!) or to policy solutions that put all eggs in the skills basket, or to redistribution programs such as the Earned Income Tax Credit (see Jared Bernstein, "Two Cheers for the Earned Income Tax Credit"). Skills and redistribution are part of a comprehensive make-work-pay program, but should not be the whole policy response. James Heckman, a respected University of Chicago economist, has calculated that relying on education and training alone to overcome the inequality trends of the past two decades would require astronomical outlays.

But it is not just a problem of cost. There are many jobs for which employment opportunities are expanding that happen to require low cognitive skill levels. Does greater educational attainment produce greater workplace-relevant skill? And in our current deregulated environment, does such investment pay off? Take child-care workers. The share of these workers with more than a high school degree increased at a spectacular rate between 1984 and 1997, from 18 to 42 percent. But their real wages declined. Other occupations that showed rapidly rising educational attainment and greater-than-average declines in wages were firefighting occupations (from 47 to 68 percent with more than a high school diploma), data-entry workers (from 38 to 58 percent), telephone operators (from 26 to 46 percent), telephone installers/repairers (from 35 to 55 percent), and electricians (from 33 to 51 percent). We should be wary about imputing much about changes in the supply of skill from educational attainment data, much less about assuming that more education, by itself, guarantees higher wages.

While low-skill wages have stabilized in the past two years, an economic slowdown will push wages down again, absent policies that address the real problem: unfettered wage competition. However, once we appreciate that the bulk of the low-wage problem can be traced to a shift in bargaining power, policy options expand dramatically. Policy makers should aim both to improve productivity (raising the ability of employers to pay) and to strengthen wage-setting institutions (reducing destructive wage competition), as well as to increase skills. The problem is not too much technology but too little. We need higher wages to encourage higher-road (higher-productivity) competitive strategies by firms. That means a higher minimum wage and a higher share of workers covered by some form of collective bargaining.

In the United States, only about 18 percent of all workers are paid wages that are set collectively, in contrast to 85–95 percent throughout Europe. While there is no need to slavishly follow the path Europe has taken, the fact is that low- and moderate-skilled workers in other developed countries have not experienced real-wage declines, much less ones close to the magnitude experienced here.

We should recognize, applaud, and build upon our current economic success—and give credit where credit is due. While economists continue to hotly debate whether the minimum wage produces negligible or just very small negative employment effects, we saw a 15 percent increase in the value of the minimum wage between 1995 and 1997. But in 2000, employers still complained of labor shortages, and the Federal Reserve still believed the economy was growing too fast. The 15 percent wage hike has apparently not caused many employment problems, but it has certainly helped those at the bottom of the wage scale. Male workers at the tenth decile finally experienced a 7.5 percent real-wage increase between 1994 and 1998, the first good news for that part of the distribution in three decades.

A higher minimum wage and a full-employment economy works. The fact is that U.S. policy makers have more latitude than most think to reestablish the modest constraints on wage competition that prevailed as recently as the 1960s and 1970s. The richest nation in the world can afford and should adopt a living-wage policy for this new millennium.

Reforming Welfare Reform

What Reform Wrought, and What Must Be Done Now

JARED BERNSTEIN AND
MARK GREENBERG

In 2002 Congress will revisit Temporary Assistance for Needy Families (TANF), often known as welfare reform. Many progressives, ourselves included, fought hard against the program that passed in 1996. We judged it too punitive and too far from the spirit of progressive reform, which would have focused less on reducing caseloads and more on both promoting employment and improving the well-being of low-income families with children. We worried that the low-wage labor market, which had been deteriorating for decades, provided little opportunity for families forced to leave public assistance. We feared that without work supports, such as child care and expanded earnings subsidies, the economic circumstances of some of our most vulnerable families would be severely diminished. We argued that the block grant funding approach of the new program revoked the important countercyclical feature of the entitlement program that TANF replaced.

So far, the evidence reveals that many of our fears have not been borne out, at least not to the extent we predicted. The labor market, particularly the low-wage sector, improved in ways we never foresaw. This, in turn, led to the first persistent real-wage gains experienced there in two and a half decades. These wage gains, the new welfare policy, and other prowork policies have attracted more low-income single mothers into paid employment. Some states, albeit too few, made considerable efforts to smooth the path to the labor market by providing the needed work supports to both the poor and near poor. And, thankfully, there has as yet been no recession.

Yet while many of our fears have not been realized, it remains the case that TANF has not focused enough on the goal of true reform: the improvement of the economic well-being of poor families with children. Caseloads have fallen sharply and employment rates have soared, but welfare reform has not fundamentally improved the living standards of many of the families it has affected. And if that was the case in the best economy in thirty years, what can we expect now that we're in a downturn?

At the heart of the TANF reauthorization debate is an assessment of the relative roles of welfare reform itself and the strong economy. This is crucial if we are to avoid over- or undercrediting the policy change. We also believe this debate should not stop at the gates of welfare reform but should address the larger question of how to lift the living standards of all working families, particularly those who have only recently benefited from the boom. These families have long responded to the personal responsibility clauses enshrined in the law that created TANF, yet their good-faith efforts are inadequately reciprocated by public obligation. So the reauthorization debate represents a historical opportunity to frame a set of policies outside of the welfare system designed to end working poverty as we know it.

Certainly, the 107th Congress may not be very receptive to a progressive set of reforms, especially since many will be arguing that the program has been an unqualified success. Yet this is a fine time to introduce a progressive agenda built around work. The core idea is that those who make a good-faith contribution to the nation's economy should never live in privation. They and their children should see their living standards rise over time, and if the market fails to deliver that result, then there is an explicit role for public policy to do so.

What Welfare Reform Did

Known as the Personal Responsibility and Work Opportunity Reconciliation Act of 1996 (PRWORA), the controversial law included far more than welfare reform. Much of it was simply designed to cut benefits or spending in low-income programs. For example, the law sharply limited the situations in which legal immigrants can qualify for public benefits, narrowed the circumstances in which children qualify for disability benefits, and imposed an array of large and small reductions in the food stamp program.

The centerpiece, though, was repeal of the Aid to Families with Dependent Children (AFDC) program and the enactment of a system of block grants to states—Temporary Assistance for Needy Families (TANF). In the block grant structure, states qualify each year for a lump sum of federal money, with most states' allocations basically frozen at 1994 or 1995 federal funding levels through 2002. With their block grants, states were expected to run time-limited, work-oriented programs of cash assistance for poor families. The law eliminated federal entitlements: No family has a federal right to assistance, and states have no obligation whatsoever to provide families with welfare benefits. States cannot use federal funds to assist families for more than sixty months (with limited exceptions) but are free to provide assistance for shorter periods. States can use their block grant funds to help families prepare for, find, and keep jobs, but states are not required to do so and can use their block grant funds for a wide array of purposes. The law created a strong incentive to cut welfare caseloads. Because there was no duty to assist families, states knew that they would get the same amount of funds whether their caseloads went up or down, and the surest way to avoid federal penalties was to bring down the state's caseload.

What was Congress trying to achieve? Different people had different goals, and the law reflects these differing views. For some, the 1996 law was largely about cutting welfare caseloads or reducing spending; for some, it was about promoting work; for some, it was about broadening state flexibility, reducing federal authority, and curtailing individual rights; and for some, it was about reducing out-of-wedlock births. For much of the public, though, the goal was that people who were able to work should do so. Many in the progressive community shared this goal but feared that the law's approach—freezing federal spending, ending individual rights, imposing time limits, creating strong incentives to cut caseloads—would mean that instead of helping parents enter and progress in the labor force, states would simply restrict assistance for families that needed help. And many progressives feared the consequences if public assistance was denied to families with the weakest labor market prospects in a low-wage labor market that was already failing many of its participants.

Throughout the 1996 debates, discussion of one goal was conspicuously lacking: There was much talk about the need to promote work and reduce welfare, but little discussion of the need to reduce poverty and promote the well-being of low-income families. Instead, both conservatives and, to a great extent, the Clinton administration created a picture in which the principal problem was seen as too many families on welfare for too long. The obvious solution was to cut caseloads by getting families to leave welfare.

Once the law was in place, states had very broad discretion in designing their policies. As a practical matter, though, most states moved in the same direction. All but two states imposed time limits on assistance, with most electing a five-year limit (about twenty set shorter time limits). Most heightened the penalties for families that missed appointments or otherwise didn't meet work-related requirements; in two-thirds of states, cash assistance can now be cut off when a family is "sanctioned" for noncompliance. Work-related activities were required, and the opportunity to participate in education and training was sharply restricted. At the same time, most states also expanded supports for families that entered low-wage jobs, by extending eligibility for welfare when a parent was employed and by increasing the availability of child care and other supports.

What Hath TANF Wrought?

In trying to understand what has happened since 1996, there are really two stories to appreciate: One concerns what has happened to families, and the other concerns what the block grant structure has meant for state budgets and spending on low-income initiatives.

When we look at the impact on families, the challenge is to disentangle the changes in welfare from those in the larger economy. Three trends are critical indicators: caseload decline, the increase in employment of poor single mothers, and the improvement in the low-wage labor market. The first two phenomena are partially related to welfare reform, while the third has occurred despite the increase in the supply of low-wage labor that welfare reform induced.

The impact most often cited is the decline in welfare caseloads. The number of caseloads began falling in 1994, but the decline greatly accelerated after the 1996 law was passed. In early 1994, 5 million families were receiving assistance. By the time the law passed, the number had fallen to 4.4 million; and by December 1999, the number was 2.4 million. In 1994, 14 percent of all children were receiving welfare benefits; by 1999 that figure had been cut by half.

But the fall in unemployment and the appearance of more and better employment opportunities in the low-wage labor market coincided with the introduction of welfare reform, raising the question of how much of the caseload decline is actually the result of welfare waivers and TANF ("waivers" were state experiments with welfare reform tried before the passage of TANF). After some debate, the current academic consensus seems to be that somewhere between 15 percent and 30 percent of the decline is attributable to welfare reform, though some estimates are higher. Of course, welfare caseloads can fall either because fewer families need help or because needy families are diverted from the rolls, and these have very different implications for evaluating the impact of reform. In fact, both dynamics are at play.

The share of poor single mothers in the paid-labor market is at an all-time high. The annual employment rates of women who received welfare benefits at some point in the year were relatively flat in the late 1980s and early 1990s. But around the mid-1990s, when welfare reform was being phased in, they took off, growing from 39 percent in 1994 to 57 percent in 1999. Of course, this was also the period when the labor market tightened up. So the challenge, again, is to figure out how much of this trend is specifically caused by welfare reform.

One useful approach is to compare the increase in work among those most likely to be affected by the policy, low-income single mothers of young children, to those less likely to be affected, namely, low-income married mothers with young kids. Such tabulations by the U.S. Department of Health and Human Services reveal that large increases in employment rates in the latter 1990s were concentrated among single mothers, not married ones. Between 1994 and 1999, low-income married moms' employment rates were unchanged at 39 percent. Those of low-income single mothers grew from that same level (39 percent) to 55 percent. Another convincing analysis (by Signe-Mary McKernan and her colleagues, available on the Urban Institute's Web site) goes further by comparing employment among these same types of women in waiver versus nonwaiver states. These authors attribute employment rate increases of six to eight percentage points over the latter 1990s to welfare reform. By their estimates, given the magnitude of the full increase in employment rates by single mothers, reform could explain as much as half of the increase.

Although this is compelling evidence of the impact of welfare reform, other developments significantly enhanced the incentive to work in the paid-labor market. During this same period in the latter 1990s, the overall unemployment rate fell from about 6 percent to 4 percent, a thirty-year low. This surge in labor demand was particularly important at the low end of the labor market. Here the decline of two percentage points translated into declines of more than ten percentage points for some disadvantaged groups of workers, such as young, less-skilled, non-college-educated African Americans, whose rate of unemployment fell from about 30 percent to 20 percent over this period. Obviously, 20 percent is still alarmingly high, but the steep decline in unemployment rates is a dramatic indicator of the benefits that accrued to minorities from the tight job market.

Along with more employment opportunities, both pretax wages and after-tax earnings of low-wage workers have increased dramatically since the latter 1990s. On the wage side, the primary factors are the tight labor market and the 1996–97 minimum-wage hike (with the former being more important). These changes led to significant real-wage gains among low-wage workers for the first time in two decades. For example, in the sixteen years between 1979 and 1995, the real wages of women earning at the twentieth percentile of income fell by 8 percent, from 1995 to 1999, it grew 8 percent, almost fully reversing the decade-and-a-half decline. Earlier in the decade, the Earned Income Tax Credit (EITC) was significantly expanded, leading to higher after-tax earnings for low-wage workers in low-income families.

Life after Welfare

To get a more precise picture of reform's impact on those who have left the welfare rolls, we need to turn to the so-called leaver studies. These projects, mostly conducted by individual states, use surveys or administrative data to track former recipients. Here are some key findings.

- At any given point in time, the majority of former welfare recipients are employed, but for many the connection to the labor market is quite tenuous. Both national and state studies find that about 60 percent of leavers are currently working, with 70 percent or more having worked at some point over the course of the year. But only about 40 percent worked consistently throughout the year. Why? Women leaving welfare tend to face more employment barriers—low skills, lack of transportation, sick or disabled children—than other populations. When they do work, however, most tend to work full time.

- Recipients who leave welfare for work earn very low wages. The studies are unanimous on this point; they document wages in the range of $6 to $8 per hour. It is too soon to tell whether the minority with solid labor-force attachment will be upwardly mobile, but the analysis done so far is not encouraging. In a compilation of nine state and local leaver studies, most involving families that left welfare in late 1996, nominal median earnings were $2,526 in the first quarter after leaving welfare and $2,821 in the fourth quarter. Another study, which followed the families that left the Wisconsin welfare rolls in late 1995, found that for those with earned income, median earnings in constant 1998 dollars were $8,608 in the first year, $9,627 in the second, and $10,924 in the third. Thus, three years after leaving assistance, median family earnings were still insufficient to reach the poverty line for a family of three ($14,150 per year).

- A significant share of leavers are not working and have very high poverty rates. Nationwide, probably about 40 percent of leavers aren't working. This group is far more likely to have limited education and work history and to run into other obstacles that make employment more difficult. Typically, the most common reason they give for not working is illness or disability. Some states have made extensive use of "sanctions"—cutting off assistance to those who don't meet attendance or other requirements. Studies of the sanctioned group consistently find that they have less education and less prior work history. A recent Michigan study found that they were also more likely to have been victims of domestic violence and more likely to be mentally ill. A three-city study found that sanctioned leavers had an 89 percent poverty rate after leaving welfare.

- After leaving assistance, many families lose their benefits under the food stamp program and Medicaid, even though they are still poor; most working leavers aren't receiving child-care subsidy assistance. Participation in the food stamp program and Medicaid drops dramatically after families leave welfare. In a national sample of families that had left welfare in the previous six months, only about half were receiving food stamps or Medicaid. Fewer than one-third of working leavers are receiving child-care subsidies. Reasons for this low participation are many: administrative mistakes, lack of information, families wanting to leave stigmatized systems that treat them badly. The net result, though, is that the support systems intended for low-earning working families aren't reaching many in need.

- Working as well as nonworking leavers often face financial deprivation after leaving welfare. Nevertheless, the majority indicate that life is better after having left. In a national study conducted by the Urban Institute, 33 percent of leavers reported that they had had to cut the size of meals or skip them entirely because there wasn't enough food; 39 percent reported that there had been a time in the last year when they had been unable to afford to pay rent, mortgage, or utilities; and 7 percent reported having had to move in with others because of inability to pay these housing costs. State studies report similar findings. At the same time, state studies consistently find that roughly half of those surveyed report that life is better since having left welfare—and that if they could choose to go back on welfare, they would not want to do so.

In sum, these studies suggest that two of the goals stated above—reducing caseloads and increasing employment—have certainly occurred. And while the strong economy has contributed, welfare reform has also played a clear role in both. But what about the most important, if least discussed, goal—improving the well-being of low-income families with children?

Here the story is at best a mixed one. The data tell us that most leavers are working but that most are not employed on an ongoing, sustained basis. The families that are working typically have higher cash incomes than they had before, but they face higher expenses (transportation, clothing, day care). At the same time, the necessary work supports—food stamps, Medicaid, and child-care subsidies—are often not reaching them. And a large minority of families—inside and outside of the welfare system—remain jobless despite the economy's unprecedented strength. Based on the evidence so far, the story is surely more positive than many anticipated in 1996. But welfare reform cannot be called an unqualified success.

How Did States Spend the Money?

In 1996, one of the most bitterly contested features of the new structure was the shift in financing from an open-ended matching program (in which federal funds matched state dollars for all allowable costs) to a block grant, whereby states would receive the same amount of federal funds each year whether their welfare caseloads went up or down. At the time, we, like many others, expressed great concern about how a block grant structure would function during a recession, when the need for assistance could be expected to escalate. We still don't know how the block grant structure will function in a recession; but providing states with constant funding while caseloads are shrinking has had a different and largely unanticipated effect: It has meant that a historically large amount of money has been made available to states not just for running their welfare programs but for financing an array of other initiatives for low-income (and in some cases, not-so-low-income) families.

Nationwide, the federal government provides states with about $16.5 billion in block grant funds each year, and states are required to spend an additional $10 billion to $11 billion in state funds in order to qualify for their block grants. Since 1994, however, the annual spending on cash assistance for poor families through the welfare system fell from $23 billion to less than $14 billion. As a result, states can now spend almost half (and in some states, far more than half) of their block grants for purposes other than cash assistance.

Where is this money going? It's impossible to get a precise picture, but it is clear that in some instances the money is funding very worthy programs. In 1999, about $3 billion in TANF funds was directed toward child care for low-income families. And some states have used their TANF funds to help establish or expand refundable earned-income tax credits, increase job-training expenditures, expand access to community colleges for low-income families, fund programs that promote individual-development accounts, expand services for victims of domestic violence, and pay for an array of other constructive ventures. At the same time, there have been examples of what has become known as "supplantation"—substituting federal funds for existing state spending and redirecting the freed-up state dollars to purposes that have little or nothing to do with helping low-income families.

So what, on balance, has implementation of the TANF block grant meant? While we can't get an exact accounting, it seems clear that as welfare spending has gone down, state spending for low-income families—particularly low-income working families—has been higher than it would have been without the block grant. In other words, while many people viewed TANF as a cut in federal spending in 1996, the effect has been the opposite, as state initiatives to help low-income working families have benefited from the available funds. At the same time, in some states, there is deep frustration, based on the sense that a significant opportunity has been missed because too little of the freed-up funding has gone to new investments to support low-income families (see Michael Massing, "Ending Poverty as We Know It").

Personal Responsibility and Public Obligation

TANF reauthorization may represent the best opportunity in the next congressional session to articulate progressive values and visions about welfare policy. To be sure, the balance of power at the federal level will limit the potential for progressive change. But we believe that what has occurred thus far can be framed in a way that builds on welfare reform's more positive aspects. Moreover, to work solely within the confines of a welfare program, however progressive, is to miss a historic opportunity to expand our vision of reform to include improvement of the social welfare of all families, not simply those leaving the welfare rolls.

The starting premise is that if the polity wants to promote work and improve the well-being of families with children, personal responsibility must be accompanied by public obligation. As the evidence has shown, most former welfare families have embraced the "PR"—the personal responsibility—in PRWORA (indeed, many had always embraced it). Millions more low-income working families never joined the welfare rolls. These families are playing by the rules; yet even in the best economy in decades, they need more help. For others, personal responsibility by itself will never lead to sustained employment without help from government. The best use of reauthorization would be to build on and expand the positive aspects of welfare reform—policies designed to ensure the economic well-being of working families—and to restructure those components of the current law that work against this goal. We also need to remember that a recession may be lurking out there somewhere, and that the legislation, as it stands, is unprepared for this looming possibility.

The reauthorization agenda should include at least these six points:

1. **Change the law's central focus from reducing caseloads to reducing poverty.** In 1996 Congress emphasized the need to cut welfare caseloads, and states responded impressively. But can states respond equally well to a national goal of reducing, and ultimately eliminating, child and family poverty? Block grant funds alone are not enough to accomplish this goal. Yet states should be required to explain how they will use block grant funds and other state resources to fight poverty, and they should be measured by their success in doing so. This does not mean a shift away from trying to promote employment: The most

straightforward way to reduce family poverty today is to help parents enter the labor force, maintain employment, and gain access to the supports that are supposed to be available to working families.

2. **Increase funding and make states more accountable for how they use their funds.** If states are being asked to broaden their focus from reducing welfare to addressing poverty, then they will need more resources, even if their welfare caseloads have shrunk. There should be continuing efforts to enhance the funding in states that receive the fewest resources in relation to their population of low-income families. At the same time, states should describe how they plan to use block grant funds, report on how they actually used them, and make a commitment that funds will not be diverted to refinance other parts of the state budget.

3. **Expand and improve the supports for low-income working families.** The availability of child-care and health-care assistance needs to be increased, and there should be a major effort to simplify and improve the accessibility of food stamps, Medicaid, and other benefits that could improve the well-being of families headed by parents in low-wage jobs.

4. **Revisit the federal time limit.** In most states, the families remaining on the welfare rolls haven't reached their time limits yet, but they soon will. There is no good reason to cut off help to families in which the parents cannot find steady work or earn enough to support a family. At minimum, time-limit rules should be revised to allow more flexibility. States should be allowed to stop the clock for working families while continuing to

provide assistance. States should also be able to provide extensions to working families and families in which a parent cannot find or maintain work. And states should be encouraged to operate publicly funded jobs programs instead of terminating assistance for families who are able to do some work but unable to maintain unsubsidized employment.

5. **Eliminate the federal bias against education and training efforts.** At the very least, it should be up to each state to decide what role education and training will play in its welfare efforts. Federal law could go further and require states to explain how they will use block grant funds to expand access to education and training programs for low-income families and how they will effectively coordinate their welfare-reform efforts with broader state strategies for workforce development.

6. **Build in economic stabilizers.** The strong economy and, in particular, the tight labor market have been central to TANF's functioning thus far. In the absence of full employment, work-based welfare reform will be severely challenged unless it ceases to depend solely on private-sector employment opportunities. The current law has a "contingency fund" intended to make additional resources available to states during an economic downturn; but, as a practical matter, the fund is structured in such a way that it will be of little or no use to all or most states. A true contingency plan for a recession (or even for a weaker labor market) would involve providing states with access to additional funding during an economic downturn and encouraging them to provide both assistance and, when needed, publicly funded employment if private-sector employment is unavailable.

Beyond TANF

The larger goal of public policy should be a transformation of the low-wage labor market and the economic prospects of the working poor. Historically, working families have been forced to turn to welfare for two reasons: first, because other systems—such as child support, unemployment compensation, the disability benefits system, and parental leave—failed or were not available; and second, because the compensation available to working parents in the low-wage labor market was insufficient to meet their families' basic needs. The next stage of welfare reform provides an opportunity to foster a broader discussion of policies that can promote work and support families. We have in mind a four-legged policy stool.

1. **Maintain full employment.** Throughout this piece, we've noted the importance of tight labor markets. Maintaining full employment is still the most effective social policy in terms of lifting the economic prospects of poor working families. Much of what we strive for pales by comparison. Yet too often progressives have treated full employment as a happy accident—as something that's outside our purview.

    The reversal of two decades of declining earnings among low-wage workers was largely a function of achieving full employment in the latter 1990s. This was no accident of fate. It stemmed largely from the actions of the Federal Reserve; the Feds' liberalized interest-rate policy allowed the unemployment rate to fall below the level that most economists had argued would trigger runaway inflation. True, other factors were at play, including a strong dollar holding down import prices and a surge in productivity growth, but other factors are always at play. It now looks as if the old speed-limit rules were not only wrong; they consigned millions of poor working families to falling real wages and incomes during the 1980s and early 1990s. We must use the reauthorization debate to enshrine full employment as our most sacred social policy.

2. **Raise pretax wages.** The minimum wage needs to be set high enough to create a reasonable floor on the low-wage labor market. Given the limited bargaining power of low-wage workers (only about 5 percent belong to unions), the minimum wage is a crucial labor market institution protecting the lowest-paid workers—who are disproportionately minorities and females—from exploitation. Of course, every time an increase is proposed, opponents trot out the argument that the increase will hurt its intended beneficiaries by pricing them out of the labor market. But reams of research now show that this is a largely bogus argument: Moderate increases in the minimum wage have almost no identifiable impact on employment. Again, the latter 1990s are an excellent example.

A much more challenging question is how high we should push the minimum wage. Though the moderate increases of the 1990s failed to generate job losses, if the minimum wage were raised high enough, negative effects would appear. Our research suggests that the minimum wage could at least be set back to its 1979 peak of $6.75 in today's dollars without generating job losses (see the minimum-wage section of the Economic Policy Institute's Web site: www.epinet.org. Reopening the indexing debate would also be worthwhile.

3. **Raise after-tax earnings.** Here the best policy by far is the EITC. It is politically popular, its antipoverty effects are well established, and it is very finely targeted at poor working families. Some problems with the EITC have recently been identified, such as the marriage penalty and the high marginal tax rate faced by those who are on the downslope of the program. But excellent plans are afoot to repair these, expand the policy, and lift the incomes of the working poor and near-poor higher still. Also, fifteen states have introduced add-on earned-income tax credits, thus allowing families that receive the federal credit to collect an additional, smaller benefit from the state. (In only ten of these cases are the credits refundable, so the benefit is unlikely to reach most of the working poor in the other five states).

At the same time, the EITC shouldn't be the only policy approach used to raise the incomes of low-earning families. Ninety-nine percent of those who receive it get it only once a year, as a lump sum; and while many families like the "forced savings" aspect of the EITC, it means that the credit does not function as a way to meet ongoing, month-to-month costs.

4. **Support work.** Regardless of a person's income, work-related expenses can be very significant. Research shows that for low-income families the costs of working can easily absorb 30 percent of family income. Given the pay scales in the low-wage labor market, the instability of employment there (which is itself related to the lack of work supports), and the lack of fringe benefits such as paid sick days or maternity leave, low-wage workers cannot meet their basic needs without help. Perhaps the most obvious barrier to steady employment for these families is child care. Transportation assistance has also proved useful, par-

ticularly in solving spatial mismatch problems in areas where the laborers can't get to the jobs. Health insurance is another obvious problem for the working poor.

Economist Randy Albelda has made the important point that along with making sure moms are job ready, we ought to make sure that jobs are "mom ready." That is, single parents—or for that matter, low-income families with two working parents—can too easily be thrown into poverty when they hit a bump in the road, whether it's a sick child, a flat tire, or the loss of a temporary job. One good idea is paid family and medical leave, perhaps financed through the unemployment insurance trust fund.

In a similar vein, advocates for the working poor have long realized that the nation's unemployment insurance program—a system designed principally with full-time working males in mind—has failed to keep pace with the evolution of either the labor market or other social policies, such as TANF. The increase in part-time and temporary work along with job instability among low-income parents, together with the loss of public assistance as an entitlement, has meant that displaced low-wage workers have nowhere to turn for support when facing a gap in paid work. Good ideas for reforming the system abound (see the Annie E. Casey Foundation's "Making Wages Work" Web site—www.makingwageswork.org—for an excellent review of them).

The last few years have witnessed some truly amazing changes in social and economic policy. A Democratic president signed a largely Republican bill that ended the entitlement of welfare and emphasized work more than any past reform effort had done. At the same time, economic conditions in the low-wage labor market improved far more than we could ever have expected.

The overlap of these two events has led to greatly reduced welfare caseloads and a lot more single mothers working in the paid labor market. That much is known. But as TANF comes up for reauthorization in 2002, a much more fundamental question must be addressed: Has welfare reform improved the well-being of poor families with children?

Our review of the evidence suggests that for some it has but for many it has not. There's more work but not much more disposable income, especially after one takes into account the expenses associated with work. For the families who haven't been able to break into the labor market, the tattered safety net is providing less help than ever. Furthermore, the TANF program, which has been greatly supported by the strong economy, is not prepared for the next recession, which seems to be edging closer by the quarter.

Yet it would be a mistake to write welfare reform off as a failure. The evidence does not support such a judgment. Some states put their surplus welfare dollars to good use, paving the way into the labor market with earnings subsidies and work supports. These programs in tandem with the tight labor market provided employment opportunities that seem to have made a real difference in the lives of former welfare recipients, many of whom report that they are happier with their lives now that they are off public assistance. It appears that these families have a sense of hope for the future that was absent in the past.

The reauthorization debate should be used to keep that hope alive and to extend it to all low-income families. To do so means fixing the program from within by strengthening the positive aspects of the welfare-to-work approach and giving states the resources and responsibility to make work pay and to sustain the gains made so far, even through the next recession. It means softening some of the punitive aspects of the program that have been shown to cause unnecessary harm to some of our most vulnerable families.

But it also means thinking beyond TANF, toward a progressive agenda tied to work that emphasizes the public obligation that should come with personal responsibility. We have framed these policies in terms of earnings and work supports, but it is early enough in the debate to begin this dialogue in earnest; new ideas may surface. Our hope is that a coalition will form—a coalition composed of those affected directly by the policy, their advocates, and their political representatives. Armed with a balanced view of TANF's impact that is based on the evidence thus far, and with a policy agenda targeted both at and beyond TANF, such a coalition can make a real and lasting difference in the lives of working Americans.

About the Contributors

ROBERT KUTTNER, who edited this book, is co-editor of *The American Prospect*. His most recent book is *Family Reunion*.

ROBERT B. REICH is currently on leave from his position as chairman of *The American Prospect* board to run for governor of Massachusetts.

HAROLD MEYERSON is executive editor of *The American Prospect*.

MICHAEL MASSING is a contributing editor for *Columbia Journalism Review* and author of *The Fix*.

JOSHUA GREEN, former staff writer at *The American Prospect*, is an editor at *The Washington Monthly*.

JON MARGOLIS is the former national political correspondent for the *Chicago Tribune* and author of *The Last Innocent Year: America in 1964*.

MARCIA K. MEYERS is an assistant professor of social work and public affairs and associate director of the Social Indicators Survey Center at Columbia University.

NANCY FOLBRE teaches economics at the University of Massachusetts and is the author of *The Invisible Heart: Economics and Family Values*.

JONATHAN COHN is a senior editor of *The New Republic* and former executive editor of *The American Prospect*.

JANET C. GORNICK teaches public policy at the City University of New York.

DAVID MOBERG is a senior editor at *In These Times*.

JOAN FITZGERALD is an associate professor of education and associate director of the Center for Urban and Regional Policy at Northeastern University.

VIRGINIA CARLSON is the research director at the Chicago Partnership for Economic Development.

NAOMI BARKO is a freelance journalist who often writes on topics concerning women.

JARED BERNSTEIN is the director of the Living Standards Program at the Economic Policy Institute and co-author of four editions of *The State of Working America*.

GORDON L. BERLIN is a senior vice president at the Manpower Demonstration Research Corporation.

DAVID HOWELL chairs the Urban Policy Analysis and Management Program at New School University.

MARK GREENBERG is senior staff attorney for the Center for Law and Social Policy.